# YO

# BREAK UP WITH YOURSELF

## *Falling in Epic Love with Your Life*

MIKAELA KOSTARAS

Mikaela Kostaras

You Can't Break Up with Yourself: Falling in Epic Love with Your Life



First edition

ISBN 978-1-7368927-0-1



Cover design by Mary Ann Smith

Interior design by Stephanie MacDougall

Editing by Alison Whyte

Publishing support by TSPA The Self Publishing Agency Inc.

# Table of Contents

## *Part IV – Commitment*

***(to All This Crazy, Not-So-Woo-Wooey-after-All Behavior That Actually Fucking Works)***



## *Part V – Faith*

***(You Must Believe Because There Is No Other Option, except to Go Back to the Old You, Which Sounds like the Worst Idea . . . Ever)***

# YOU CAN'T BREAK UP WITH YOURSELF

## *Falling in Epic Love with Your Life*

# Everyone Deserves Epic Love

The stories in this book are V. real, and real stories aren't always the easiest to read. In fact, some of the accounts may be triggering for you. Thank you for following my journey—a journey I now recognize I was fortunate to face with a privilege I often took for granted.

While you read, I'd like you to think about two life-changing lessons I learned along the way:

1. Pain can lead to purpose.
2. Mistakes can lead to breakthroughs.

I have written this book from my own perspective. In other words, the stories within are told from the point of view of a white, heterosexual, cis female. I wholeheartedly respect all communities, but I can only write from my own experience. That said, I firmly believe the insights I share are universal, and I hope that everyone who reads this book, regardless of their identity, will find them useful. After all, love is love, and we *all* deserve it.

# Introduction—
# The (Not So) Shocking Reason I Was Still Single

*It is only when you take responsibility for your life that you discover how powerful you truly are.*
*—Allanah Hunt*

Despite being less than six months over legal voting age in the United States, I had already fallen victim to four traumatic events. I was never quite the same, and I experienced negative ripple effects—notably in my romantic relationships—for years. Ten years, to be exact.

A decade after my final teenage tragedy—after enduring back to back (to back) failed relationships—I found myself crying desperately on the kitchen floor of my lackluster yet over-priced one-bedroom apartment. I was wine drunk at five o'clock in the evening and watching episode number who-the-hell-knows of *Scandal* on Netflix. The cringiest part about said turmoil was that it was caused by yet another Joe frickin' Schmoe I had met on yet another dating app. He broke my hanging-on-by-a-thread heart the moment he (finally) made it crystal clear he wasn't looking for anything serious. Homeboy was looking for a friend with the best kind of benefits—not an exclusive, long-distance relationship with a girl he didn't exactly know too well. Meanwhile, I was privately planning detailed logistics of a cross-country move for a guy I spoke to exclusively via texts and FaceTime calls, usually in the late hours of the evening. It should have been obvious and now I can clearly see the writing was on the wall for this faux-lationship; but at the time, I was rattled to the core. What's a *faux-lationship*? It's one where you think it's a relationship or leading to a relationship when, in fact, the other party is solely interested in having a "good time."

Between my exasperated blubbers and gulps of two-dollar Cabernet, I wondered how, yet again, I could have been so wrong. This encounter wasn't the first, second, or even third time I had convinced myself someone who was:

a) donned head to toe in nothing but red flags

and

b) just not that into me

was my star-crossed soulmate. In fact, I had been adopting this mindset since the age of sixteen when I fell in "love" with my co-worker from Jamba Juice. He was going to be my forever. We were going to live happily ever after, of course, since there's nothing a sixteen-year-old knows more about than a serious relationship. Needless to say, *Mr. Jamba Juice* was *not* my forever person, and we did not get married following high school graduation. Regardless, I grew up in a world filled with Nicholas Sparks novels and Hallmark movie endings, so I was sure that my soulmate was out there somewhere; however, my adult reality was less Prince Charming and more evil stepmother keeping me from the ball. More than a decade later, I was still determined to find my epic love but continued to fall short. Romance, for me, was anything but a fairy tale.

There I was, wallowing in self-pity because a boy didn't like me back as if I were a hormonal teenager in P.E. class (we'll return to high school P.E. later in this book). I wished hell on this guy for being such a jerk. Naturally, my girlfriends rallied around me proclaiming, "You were too good for him anyway," "You're better off without him," or my personal favorite, "That asshole totally led you on!" Amid my cheap wine buzz, I came to a chilling realization: this wasn't about him or any of the (several) others before him.

**It was about me.**

I felt like I was the sole audience member in my own metaphorical movie theater watching an impressively crappy film about my love life. I'm confident Roger Ebert would have preferred to watch all three *Fifty Shades of Grey* movies back to back rather than tune in to twenty minutes of my biopic: *The Fuckboys of My Past*. Every past relationship and hook-up were playing on screen and I couldn't help but scream at the main character (me): "But . . . he smokes cigarettes? You can't stand that!" or "Really . . . you're going to give the guy who cheated on you (multiple times) another chance?!" I sat in complete horror, half stunned and half mortified, because I kept making the same mistakes over and over again. How could I have let this go on for so long? The number of questionable choices I made in the name of L-O-V-E over the years was preposterous. The most astonishing thing, however, was the complete lack of L-O-V-E I had for *myself*.

I wish I could say the other parts of my life were firing on all cylinders but, unfortunately, my dating life was not the only area that needed improvement. I barely had five dollars to my name after I paid for rent, utilities, groceries, my dog's food, and student loans. I was working a job that made me cry ev-er-y Sunday night because the thought of returning the next morning was unbearable. I had issues with some members of my family, and I had let most of my friendships fizzle. Let's just say this movie about my life wasn't worthy of an Oscar, let alone a spot on Bravo TV . . . or even (shudders) TLC.

Although I had been the victim of some serious trauma, I had been playing the role of a victim of life and love for far too long. I wasn't the only person in the world who went on terrible first dates, stayed in toxic relationships that lasted years too long, worked jobs that made her Miserable (with a capital M), or experienced devastating personal events. But I was acting like I had zero control over these things and my reactions to them. Sure, the Universe's sense of humor can be quite, ahem, interesting (to say the least), but we are always in control of ourselves, even when it doesn't feel like it. Things may not be your fault, but that sure as hell doesn't mean they should derail you from what should be your number one priority: to be genuinely happy. It was about damn time I recognized that I *did* have control over my life, and I needed to own it. I just needed to figure out, you know, *how*.

By this point, I had begun to sober up, but I was still sitting on the tiles of my kitchen floor. At that pivotal moment, I decided to change no matter what it took. There was just one problem: I had absolutely zero idea where to start. Unfortunately for me, Mr. Forever didn't miraculously walk into my life the next morning with a magical hangover elixir, one perfect for curing the inevitable morning-after-cheap-wine headache we all know and despise (although my very own Mr. Forever *did* walk into my life a little bit later).

If you made the decision to buy a book about how to quit dating the wrong people and find the epic love of your dreams, you are likely looking for a change. You're tired of the games, the tears, and the ghosting. You want to feel truly happy and at peace. You want to find your forever partner. I'm also confident your family and friends (who are probably all happily married or engaged and have no clue which direction to swipe on Bumble) won't leave you alone about being single and bring it up every time you see them. I've been there. Don't even get me started on how much I used to dread holidays and other family gatherings.

Taking ownership of your life and your emotions isn't something you learn in school. Reframing and redefining everything you've been telling yourself for years isn't easy; but, I assure you, owning it is ab-so-fuck-ing-lute-ly essential to attracting not only your forever person, but also—and most importantly—finding *yourself.* You know, the *real* you behind all the masks and filters you use on Instagram and TikTok. In order to take ownership and find yourself, you have to be willing to put in the w-e-r-k, just like I have to train abs multiple times a week to try to look a little more like Gabrielle Union (who is twenty years my senior and somehow still looks younger than me). It took me several years of reading, reflecting, writing, crying, listening, and therapy (not to mention copious amounts of wine) to begin to understand the significant role our mindset plays in, well, everything; and how we all have the power within ourselves to make every dream we have—whether it's meeting our soulmate (raises hand), securing a dream job, buying a dream car, or whatever it may be—a reality that makes you so damn happy you could scream out in glee.

Every single facet of your dream life *is* possible and waiting to become a reality if you believe that it is, in fact, possible. I know. This seems much easier said than done when the Bank of America app giggles whenever you open it, your dating app matches exclusively consist of Christinas who can't carry on a conversation or Chads who think *The Wolf of Wall Street* is the best movie ever made, and the only car you can purchase with all cash is a Matchbox.

I'm happy to report I was able to embrace, understand, and apply the stupidly simple (yet sometimes incredibly complicated) concepts I present in this book in my own life. I had to not only recognize, but also understand the *root* of my issues and the mistakes I made as a result. Once I committed to a future without them and a steadfast love for myself above all else, I met and married the man of my dreams. Yes, the same self-loathing girl who sobbed about a lost Tinder "love" on her kitchen floor met and married her forever person, who just happens to be a wickedly handsome, charismatic, and supportive man who looks like a Greek god and fills up my wine glass without being asked. More important than falling in love with someone else, I learned to truly fall in love with myself—and my life. I guess you could say I got my Hallmark movie ending after all; but this movie had a radically different plot, an inspired director, and a powerful producer.

The insider knowledge I'm going to give you can also go way beyond fixing a crappy love life. On top of finding my very own Mr. Forever, I was able to quit my corporate job with a sense of peace and certainty to finally begin doing work that excites me to my core. I went from being bankrupt to seeing more zeros in my bank account than I ever thought possible. The good news is this is something that can absolutely happen for you, too. Trust me on this. Although I love Britney Spears, "lucky" is not a word I would use to describe myself. **Luck has nothing to do with this.**

I want you to live the life of your dreams and wake up every morning next to the sexiest human on the planet—the person who sets your soul on fire. I want you wake up with a desire to make this dream life even better because you believe in your heart that you deserve a life you can celebrate every day of the week. Not only do I want this for you, but I also *know* it is possible. Your success, in dating and beyond, is inevitable! Your success has been waiting for you since the day you were born. That's something worth popping the bubbly for, right? (As if we need another reason to pop some bubbly these days beyond the fact we somehow made it through 2020 in one piece.)

I want to be clear that I'm not a matchmaker or a licensed therapist, but I do have a fuck ton of experience in doing everything you *shouldn't* do when trying to meet the love of your life. This book won't offer a single mathematical formula to fix all your dating woes—although a formula (even though I really hate math) would have saved me a lot of time, energy, money, and tears. This book also isn't going to teach you a quick and easy way to get a ring on your (or someone else's) finger; however, if you follow along and incorporate these principles into your own life, you may have a sparkly diamond in your future—if you desire that sort of thing, of course.

My hope is that in reading along my journey across a few good men (actually, many were jerks), several chuckle-inducing decisions, and my personal awakening, you will become unapologetic about the life and epic love you deserve. My wish is that you read with an open heart and mind, laugh a little, cry a ton, and see if you identify with any of the setbacks I encountered on and beyond the dating scene. Be as honest as possible with yourself, especially when it doesn't feel amazing. If you find yourself thinking something along the lines of: "Oh shit. I've done that. Maybe I should change . . .", make a promise to yourself to commit to change and be relentless in the pursuit of your happiness.

Finally, for the love of truffle fries, **learn to love *yourself* before anyone and anything else.** The most important relationship in your life isn't the one you have with your partner, your family, or your friends. It's the one you have with yourself. This one connection will impact the quality of every other relationship in your life. Don't worry, we'll get to that, too. It's often the most challenging relationship of them all because there's one person in this life you can never break up with: yourself.

# Part I
# Reflections

**(of a Frustrated Single Woman Who Might Die If She Sees One More #ENGAGED Post on Her Instagram Feed)**

# Chapter 1—
# Heartbreak Hurts, but It Doesn't Last Forever

*The heart will break, but broken live on.*
*—Lord Byron*

For most of my young adult life, I was the kind of girl who would shy away from eye contact—particularly eye contact with cute strangers. What I didn't realize was this habit was rooted in a seriously bad case of extremely low, practically non-existent self-worth that will be heavily evident throughout many chapters of this book. If a scientist were to combine equal parts of total introvert and negative self-worth, I'd come out on the other side of the conveyor belt.

Why would a cute boy be looking at me? Do I look okay? Did I wear the right outfit? But . . . that girl over there is way prettier and has bigger boobs than me. All I have is a weird dimple on the left side of my face and a tooth that never grew in right.

Those are just a few examples of the incredibly silly and often self-deprecating thoughts that would run through my anxious mind the moment someone looked in my direction. More than the anxiety I experienced wondering what other people were thinking about me when they weren't thinking about me at all, I found eye contact with men—especially of the sexy variety—quite unnerving.

It was as if I thought these beautiful creatures were going to look right into my soul and instantly know all my deepest, darkest secrets. And I totally didn't want that. Or did I? (Ultimately, I kind of did—but just not instantaneously.)

I'll never forget the night I met the guy who I like to call *Sir L. B.* At the time, I was in my early twenties living in California at my parents' house, hating every second of it, not being remotely appreciative of the privilege I was afforded, and trying to start over after a royally epic false start at college. One of my good friends at the time invited me to go out to a local bar for college night, so I did the whole to-go-or-not-to-go back and forth banter in my head, finally agreeing to go in hopes of escaping my own thoughts for an hour or two. Unhealthy behavior number one: drinking alcohol to avoid lingering difficult emotions. **I assure you that everything—seriously, ev-er-y-thing—is worse when you're hungover.**

Surprisingly, my impromptu night at the local country music joint ended up being a lot more fun than I expected. I was enjoying myself, drinking with friends, and dancing (or at least attempting to) for what seemed like the first time in a V. long while. There I was, locking eyes with a dreamy stranger standing on the other side of the dance floor—a dance floor riddled with attractive college-age girls in cut-off shorts and cowboy boots. He was excruciatingly handsome, but in an understated kind of way. Wearing a simple white t-shirt, ball cap, and just-the-right-amount-of-tight blue jeans, his bluer-than-the-Mediterranean eyes pierced deep into my soul like icicles spearing the night air on a crisp, northeastern winter evening. The craziest part of our encounter was I couldn't even imagine trying to look away. I felt pulled to him in a way I had not felt before. Miss I'm-not-that-weird-but-I-can't-look-cute-men-in-the-eye Mikaela was holding a gaze with this hottie across the bar. Did I just have an out-of-body experience?

In a million years, I would have never expected him to ask me to dance considering the fifty other (very pretty) girls not-so-patiently waiting to be asked to two-step. In my personal version of *Footloose*, he turned out to be the best dancer in the bar, had an amazing smile capable of melting even the iciest of hearts (i.e., mine), and was genuinely one of the nicest guys I had ever met in California. While I'm sure there are plenty of great California boys, my experience was mostly that of the absent-minded, surf-obsessed, and disinterested-in-anything-serious kind of boys. Of course, Sir L. B. offered to drive me home that night to my parents' house. I was more than confident the fact that my place of residence was my childhood bedroom would be the end of our dreamy affair; but if it had been the end, he certainly wouldn't have his own chapter in this very book.

Sir L. B. was the epitome of a Texas gentleman who seemingly walked straight out of a Nicholas Sparks novel and waltzed into my not-so-novel-worthy life. Beyond the good looks and natural charm, he opened my door (gasp!), took me out on dates (double gasp!!), paid for everything (triple gasp!!!), and generally opened my eyes to a kind of dating experience unlike any I had ever encountered. He lived in a much wealthier area than I did, had a cool, adult job, and wore luxurious clothes. I remember thinking he was the first guy I dated who had his shit together. My bar for a prospective partner was so low that finding a grown man who had a car, a house, a job, and paid his own bills was the greatest thing I could have ever imagined. I realize the ability to function independently as an adult should be the baseline expectation for a potential romantic interest, but clearly, my relationship standards needed some improvement.

After a few months of the same pattern of dates, phone calls, and sleepovers, I inevitably grew restless. We've all been there, right? You know, when you're left wondering the proverbial dating question of "Are we . . .?"

PSA: If you are wondering if you are or you aren't with someone, you have already answered your question. I assure you—no matter who the person is or what their sexual orientation is—when someone wants to be with you, they will be with you exclusively. No questions asked. You should never, under any circumstances, stay with someone in hopes that they will one day feel the same way as you. Never. I'm here to remind you that you deserve someone who sees you for the amazing person you are right now. Not five months or five years from now. Now!

Obviously, we weren't in an exclusive relationship (because, you know, we never defined the relationship). But I really wanted to be. There was no question this dude liked me enough to keep me in the picture; however, just because someone likes you, it doesn't necessarily mean that person wants to be in a relationship with you. I won't deny that it feels awesome to get attention from someone you're interested in, but I can confirm it won't continue to feel so good when you find out that person isn't interested in the same end goal as you. It was clear he was not interested in a committed relationship. He was a flirt who wanted attention from as many girls as possible. This is a fact. Did I ignore this fact because he talked to me daily and took me out on awesome dates? Abso-fuckin'-lutely.

Remember the bar where we first locked eyes? Well, that neighborhood watering hole became my new go-to spot—an unexpected haven of sorts. Seriously, many of my friends can attest I went there six nights a week (only because it was closed on Mondays). And one to two nights a week, I would see Sir L. B. there, where he would treat me like just another girl on the dance floor. I couldn't possibly be just another girl, right? We had an amazing date less than twenty-four hours ago so he's totally playing hard to get, right? Wrong! I was, in fact, Just. Another. Girl.

After about five months of this confusing behavior, I got fed up and did what most of us have done at some point in our lives: I gave him the good ole ultimatum. You know, that "fun" talk every person on this planet hates. The one where you stand up for yourself and say, "Listen here, either we're in a relationship, or we're not." In short: commit or split!

I did this secretly hoping I would have the fairy tale ending I had seen play out so many times on screen and paper: the *Sixteen Candles*-esque finale; the part where the guy realizes how absolutely amazing the girl was all along, admits he's been an idiot, and begs her to take him back; the part where they ride off into the sunset, drink piña coladas, and live happily ever after while unicorns dance in the background. There's a reason this type of scene exists solely in books and movies—because (say it with me): **books and movies aren't like real life.** Hell, reality shows aren't even like real life.

The story actually ended with me devastated and sobbing in the bar's parking lot and then at home in my mom's arms. I wondered what was wrong with me and why he didn't feel the same way. If only time travel were real, I would go back to that exact moment, bring myself a shot of tequila, and tell that swollen-faced girl that it wasn't about her at all. He simply didn't want a relationship. The only problem about this was that I failed to recognize it and accept it before my little heartstrings got involved. It didn't help that I continued to see Sir L. B. for many months to come (you know, because we frequented the same bar), but I tried to pretend that his ability to flirt with anyone with two legs and a vagina didn't bother me to my core. Newsflash: it totally bothered me, but I did become an amazing dancer, so at least there was a silver lining.

In a case of modern dating karma, Sir L. B. slid into my DMs a few years later when I was living in a different city and he was living in a different country on the other side of the world. I was long over him and in another relationship that was (unbeknownst to me) on its last legs. He was living in Bali and sent me a surprisingly long message explaining that I had remained on his mind despite the years gone by, and that while he hadn't been ready at the time of my ultimatum, he now realized he had made a huge mistake. I guess you *can* get the *Sixteen Candles* ending—you just have to wait a while.

The most interesting part of his message was something totally unexpected and unrelated to a rekindling of our romance (although, romance and a second chance were definitely the things he was seeking): he asked me what I was doing with my life. He didn't understand how I got to where I was (working a shitty job I hated with my entire being) or why I was there (living in a place I'd always hated). He mentioned our previous conversations about traveling, doing big things, and changing the world for the better. Yet here

I was in corporate America, living soullessly in a not-so-great relationship. The worst part? He was spot freakin' on. Who would have thought that Sir L. B. had learned so much about me in such a short time? Not me, that's for damn sure. I guess there is something to be said about eye contact and looking into someone's soul after all.

Most of us have grown up with the notion that second chances—or third, fourth, even seventeenth in the case of *Sex and the City*—always end well. I mean, if Carrie and Big can end up together, anyone is worth a second chance at love, right? Almost every romantic comedy or drama out there has some sort of arc in which a character realizes their mistake and pines for forgiveness, with the end result of a romantic reunion. It's tied neatly into a bow. Modern dating, however, is anything but neat. It's messy and confusing. And sometimes—even if the person deserves it—you don't want to give your ex (or, in my case, fuckboy-of-the-past-turned-emotionally-available man) a second chance.

Or, if you're like me in the case of Sir L. B., sometimes you do.

Flash forward a few months to when we're both back home in San Diego, and we mutually decide to go out on a date. Isn't it interesting how time can change your perception about things? While I still could recognize and appreciate what a handsome and amazing guy he was, I was no longer attracted to him. We spent a wonderful evening together that ended in a moonlit kiss by the beach, which would have made the old me melt like a rosé popsicle in a scorching Vegas summer. But melt I did not. I had no clue how he felt about the date, but I have to admit, I enjoyed not caring.

I wish that all unrequited love stories ended like this one—with the rejected lover ultimately getting the upper hand—but sadly, this often isn't the case. This is also not the point (although I won't lie, it felt really good). The point is: when you're feeling shitty, unloved, unsexy, and every other negative emotion after someone turns you down, **it's okay to be sad.** You must feel whatever emotions come up and work through them because emotions are like children: they just need to be heard. You might obsess about it because you're human, and as humans, we ~~need~~ want answers. **Sometimes you have to move on without getting any fucking answers.** This is a ridiculously hard lesson to learn—especially if you deserve a reason why—but important for your emotional survival.

Whether you have the answers or you don't, there will come a day, without a shadow of a doubt (I would legitimately give up wine for the rest of my life to bet you on this very fact) when it won't bother you anymore. One day, you won't think about that person anymore. You won't look them up on social media or wish that there was a text from them when you wake up. If you're like me, there will be one day when you'll wonder what the hell you were so obsessed about in the first place. That's what you need to remind yourself of when the emotions are overwhelming, and you're left wondering what the hell happened. One. Freakin'. Day. You will not give a flying you-know-what because you will be doing just fine without them.

# Chapter 2— Dating Down and Leveling Up: The Problem with Falling in Love with Someone's Potential

*Some people are settling down, some people are settling and some people refuse to settle for anything less than butterflies.*
*—Candace Bushnell*

Ah, to be twenty again. Raise your hand if you'd like to rewind ten plus years knowing everything you know now. It's a tempting thought, isn't it? Aside from the tighter waistline and ability to drink everything in sight without a hangover lasting the next three business days, there are a boatload of surprisingly great things about being young and dating all the wrong people. I never quite realized (or bothered to appreciate) this until I reminisced about the most influential relationships of my past love life. The biggest realization of all: you will always be young enough *not* to be jaded by past relationships and faux-lationships alike.

Before I grew up into a struggling-not-to-be-jaded-but-still-kinda-jaded-twenty-something with a serious affinity for fuckboys, I was relatively inexperienced in the dating world. I had been through two high school faux-lationships and college was certainly *not* turning out to be the place I could find a boyfriend. So, I went for the next best thing: falling for my older co-worker, of course! By the way, "next best thing" is a euphemism for a terrible decision. Luckily, your twenties are meant for football fields of terrible decisions, so at least I was doing something right.

I was working in a brand-new Mexican restaurant when I met him—*Mr. Bartender*. He was just shy of a decade older than me, but if we measured age by emotional maturity, I'd probably have been at least two decades older than him. That seemingly small detail didn't matter to me at the time because I was focused on other more important things; I loved how outgoing he was (why do introverts fall for extroverts . . . *why?*), the fact that everyone seemed to like him, and the way he would saunter over to the hostess stand with a silly grin to compliment my green eyes. You know, the kinds of things that make an impressionable twenty-year-old V. weak in the knees. It was like I was the dorky high school freshman, wearing the ugliest thick glasses and a smile full of braces, while he was the senior football star with a full ride to Stanford in the fall. In reality, he was very much *not* the hotshot I considered him to be.

I ignored the fact that he was pushing middle age, spending all his money on weed, living with questionable roommates, and regularly not waking up until two o'clock in the afternoon (and *that* was an early alarm). Being the young, naive, and incredibly impressionable girl I was, I regularly chauffeured him around in my car, bought and brought him dinner, and drove to his apartment at one o'clock in the morning for the sake of "romance." I did all the things any self-respecting person would do. Just kidding! I did exactly *the opposite* of what any self-respecting person would do, which would have been to recognize that this was someone who was not capable of a serious relationship at that time and move on. In other words, **I was settling.** My friends knew it, my parents knew it, hell—even some strangers probably knew it. But I settled because my standards were low, and my self-worth was even lower. Why? Don't worry, we'll dive into *that* topic later.

If we're being really honest with ourselves, how many of us are guilty of settling—especially when it comes to our romantic relationships? I'm willing to bet that the majority of us are V. guilty. It's so easy for us to recognize when those around us are guilty as charged, but when it comes to recognizing it within ourselves, we aren't *quite* so talented. Why do we continue to settle when we're worth so much more? Why do we continue to give our precious time to potential mates who are exclusively clothed in nothing but red flags? Why do we ignore our biggest non-negotiables for the sake of a hottie (who also happens to be emotionally immature and very much unavailable)?

Honestly, there could be an entire book dedicated to this very question because we all have our unique reasons. You could be like me and suffer from a bad case of low self-worth, thinking that you aren't worthy of anything better than what's in front of you. Maybe the physical chemistry you have with someone is out of this world, and you can't seem to let that go even though everything else is totally lackluster. Perhaps you see this person for what they *could* be rather than for who they actually *are*. (Where are my fellow fixers at?) Or you might be scared—terrified of being alone or worried that there just isn't anything better out there.

Regardless of your reasons, you deserve a life where you don't feel like you are settling or need to settle. We all should be reaching for the stars—going after the very best for no other reason than we are *all* deserving of, you guessed it, the very best. We deserve this in our relationships, friendships, careers, ev-er-y-thing. Your personal list of non-negotiables in a partner exists for a reason. Make a promise to yourself to not let anything or anyone make you feel like you need to waver from it. While chemistry is a piece of the puzzle, it is not the whole damn thing. I will advocate for sexiness and physical attraction in romantic relationships until I am blue in the face, but we need a hell of a lot more than someone who gets us tingling between the legs to make us *fully* happy. If your primary focus is on physical attraction, you may miss out on the kind of people who will fulfill your mind and heart as much as your body. It's time to stop dating down and start leveling the fuck up, okay?

While Mr. Bartender was a ton of fun and our time together was full of laughs, I'm confident you aren't the slightest bit surprised a serious relationship didn't develop from our string of superficial encounters. Don't worry, I too was not shocked he wasn't my guy as our "dates" consisted of midnight walks around the bay while smoking a joint or going to 7-Eleven to buy candy before watching a movie at his place. He only gave me a miniscule amount of his attention while I gave him *all* of mine. A lack of attention is not something you'll experience in epic love.

Of course, an amazing date doesn't necessarily require an expensive steakhouse with $300 bottles of wine. Let's remind ourselves of the actual purpose of dating: to find out if you like someone enough to be in a relationship with them (it shouldn't be to get a free meal or a way to take your mind off someone else). If someone genuinely likes you, I promise you, that person *will* make an effort, especially if you won't accept anything less. Standards: they are a V. good thing. You *are* worth it. This doesn't mean that a meal shared together at McDonalds can't be just as special as a date at Mastro's steakhouse. It's the intention that counts more than the number of dollar signs next to the restaurant name on Yelp.

Mr. Bartender and I didn't have a nasty falling out. One day, it just sort of stopped (it also helped that I enrolled full-time back in college, so I couldn't stay up into the wee hours of the morning smoking weed anymore—not if I didn't want to fail for a second time, that is). Even as I'm sitting here reminiscing about our time together, it's hard to remember how I felt about it. It was like one day he was there, and the next he wasn't. Time, yet again, seems to have healed those wounds. Or maybe I'm just losing my memory now that I'm the one approaching middle age.

While I assure you this is not a central theme of my relationship past, Mr. Bartender came traipsing back into my life almost a decade later thanks to, yet again, the power of social media. It made me infinitely happy to see that the emotionally immature and financially irresponsible bartender I had so fondly begun my twenties with had finally grown into the man I always knew he could be. He decided to leave the bar industry life for good and generally just seemed to, you know, grow the hell up. One of my biggest strengths (and equally biggest weaknesses) has always been the ability to clearly see *the potential* in people rather than who they are at that moment in time. Falling in love with someone's potential can be both the easiest and most painful way to get your heart broken. I knew Mr. Bartender had it in him, so to actually see that come to life (albeit a decade later), made me beyond proud.

Unfortunately, certain people take longer to mature than others. Age often has little to do with it. It takes more time for some people to sow their wild oats, get it out of their system, and decide they're ready to settle down. Sometimes this happens intentionally, and other times it happens when they meet the person who makes them want to finally, ahem, change. If the person you're seeing exhibits bad behavior, won't change for you, and/or is clearly not emotionally mature *and* available, it might be time to check on your standards to ensure you're not settling. I don't care how dreamy the person is, how good they are in bed, or that they check off other boxes. If the person you're seeing isn't emotionally available and mature, it's going to be V. difficult to have a lasting relationship together that isn't riddled with toxicity.

Mr. Bartender, turned *the boy who finally grew the hell up*, wanted a second chance with me. I must give some serious kudos to the dude because he was really persistent about making that happen. He wrote to me daily, took a genuine interest in getting to know more about me, planned visits to see me, and sent me a beautiful bouquet for my birthday. He really did everything right, except it was the second time around, and honestly just a little too late. Maybe if I had been in a better headspace or in a different zip code, we could have tried, but ultimately, the timing simply wasn't right. We still had chemistry and were seemingly emotionally aligned, but we were in two different places—literally and figuratively.

To be clear—this is *not* a PSA advising against giving someone another chance. Hell, I've been given second chances by people who had no business forgiving me, so I'm V. grateful and don't take this issue lightly. That said, giving someone a second chance should always be a deliberate decision based on a careful consideration of the particular situation (not just the fact that your ego feels vindicated). Love can make us be many things, including impulsive and stupid, so we all could use a little help to strengthen our minds as well as our hearts. Just because someone wants you back does not necessarily mean you should take that person back. If someone from your past wants you back and your entire being screams "Yes!" like I did with Sir L. B., then go for it. The worst that can happen is, you know, what already happened between you. The decision is up to you.

Looking back, I clearly understand that the Universe was conspiring in my favor and that while Mr. Bartender ended up becoming the man I knew he could be, it didn't happen at the right time *for me*. This is a wonderful reminder for all of us that we are always on the right path. This is referred to as divine timing, which is the idea that everything that takes place in your life happens exactly how and when it needs to happen. The beauty of heartbreak, or in this case, a fizzling of some youthful lust, is that broken relationships with the wrong people at the wrong time teach us something and can prepare us for the *right* person. The good thing about meeting Mr. Bartender when I did was that our time together helped me identify (albeit many, many years later) some self-worth issues. I realized my relationship picker tended to seek out men I could help reach their fullest potential instead of men who were already there, and that settling is something I (and every other human on the planet) should never, ever do—particularly when it comes to romantic relationships.

If I had met him later in life, I might not have learned these lessons and perhaps I might have been the one who had a little growing up to do. The beauty of our relationship these days is that I actually consider Mr. Bartender a good friend; so good, in fact, he is very much aware of his chapter in this book and has been one of the most supportive people throughout the challenging process of writing down my experiences. Clearly, the Universe had other plans for the young girl who fell for the popular bartender at her hostess-with-the-mostess job. When you begin to not only understand, but also *believe* that every relationship comes into your life for a reason, you can find gratitude even for the crappiest relationships. Trust me—you're always in the right place at the right time and every relationship has some sort of purpose (even when it doesn't feel like it).

# Chapter 3— Vulnerability Sucks: Don't Date a Dreamy DJ If You Aren't Willing to Be Un-Dreamy

*To share your weakness is to make yourself vulnerable; to make yourself vulnerable is to show your strength.*
*—Criss Jami*

Some relationships teach you a lot about yourself, other relationships teach you a lot about relationships, and some simply teach you a few life lessons you've probably been ignoring for far too long. My relationship with the man I fondly refer to as *Smooth Operator* happened to teach me all three.

I met Smooth Operator at a nightclub—not the place I was expecting to find true love. My thoughts were more in line with "I'll kiss that guy over there for a free drink." I wish I was kidding, but I am guilty of flirting with guys at bars for the sake of a $15 vodka soda I didn't have to pay for. That said, I must have been giving off some serious RiRi vibes that evening, because I found love in a hopeless place. That, or "Pon de Replay" was playing in the background. Can't remember—too many vodka sodas.

If Smooth were an order at Starbucks, he would be a Venti Caramel Macchiato, *with extra caramel.* This man was Fine, and sweet like sugar (minus the headache). Besides having good genetics on his side, he was also kind of a big deal. Smooth was a local—and quite popular—DJ. And, as it turned out, he thought I was hot, too. What a time to be alive! The most shocking part was that he turned out to be an incredibly kind and normal guy, despite his career of choice and the party lifestyle associated with it. While he did have crazy stories of partying with Lil Jon and plenty of other V. famous folks, he was actually a stable introvert who had a sincere passion for making music. Originally an East Coast boy, now living on the other coast, he asked me out on a date (of the real variety) the very morning after we met. This is what dreams are made of!

Smooth took me to an ah-mazing Italian restaurant (Italian happens to be my favorite), ordered me red wine (at this point, I didn't even care if he was somehow reading my mind), laughed at my jokes, asked me intriguing questions, and, well, you get the picture. We both were hooked from the very first date. Date #1 turned into Date #15 (or whatever number; we went on a lot of dates, okay?), and we ended up spending a lot of time together. Somehow though, I always managed to keep a safe emotional distance. This was easy to do as both of our jobs required us to work weekend nights—nights other couples might spend out on the town or staying in and cuddling while watching Netflix.

Ultimately, this schedule worked for us. At the time, I was planning weddings, so going out on weekend nights before midnight wasn't possible for me. I was too busy making sure the drunk maid of honor knew where to stand when it was time for her speech at the reception. And Smooth was busy turning tables at whatever nightclub he was DJing at for the night. Yet, through a string of mid-week date nights, a mutual love of hockey, and endlessly easy conversation, we started to form a V. special bond.

For the first time in my life, a genuinely great guy wanted to make things official with me when I, too, felt the same way. Gone were the days of ultimatums or wondering where my relationship stood. Smooth came out and told me what I had only dreamed of being a reality. In his own words, he quietly informed me he didn't want to date anyone else and didn't want to even *think* of me dating anyone but him. Few things feel better than having someone who you are super interested in say this to your face. As mentioned in chapter 1, if someone wants to be with you, they will make it V. clear that they do, in fact, want to be with you exclusively. On a somewhat ironic side note, this intimate conversation happened at midnight in the middle of a loud nightclub—but, hey, it happened nonetheless. Again, it must have been the RiRi vibes. I'm kidding (kind of).

I finally found myself in the most normal and healthy relationship I had ever been in. The kind of epic relationship I so desperately wanted was mine. I even introduced the guy to my parents, which for me was a V. big deal. Introducing any guy to my parents had always been the last thing I wanted to do. My parents are my biggest cheerleaders, and I never want to disappoint them. Deep down, I think I subconsciously knew many of the guys I dated would disappoint me (and in turn, them), so I just stopped talking about my relationships and delayed the whole meeting-the-parents deal as long as possible. When I did introduce someone to my mom and dad, I certainly didn't make a big deal of it; but Smooth met them with ease. It was a flawless interaction. I'm sure if you asked my mom about it today, she would tell you she thought I would marry the guy, or at least hoped I would. *Mrs. Mikaela Smooth Operator.*

Those are some big shoes to fill and I, despite my obsession with all things shoes, was *not* ready for that type of pressure. What does someone who feels overwhelmed by how fantastic someone is and the potential of a relationship becoming something beyond just dating do? A person who had worked through their trauma(s) would simply focus on being happy in the relationship and communicate their needs. At the time, I don't even think I could give a definition of trauma (much less face what I needed to face), so I did what I had always done when things got too much for me to handle and I felt scared of the unknown: self-sabotage.

When I look back on my relationship with Smooth, I was most afraid of him not loving me anymore or leaving me as soon as I showed any of my flaws. You see, despite my self-esteem issues, I can *seem* like an extremely confident gal. To bring the zodiac into it: I'm a classic Aries: fiery, confident, and V. independent. But Aries people are also extremely sensitive and emotional creatures. Basically, we're hard on the outside, but soft on the inside—like the perfect French fry! Unfortunately, I never allowed Smooth to see that soft part. Can you imagine not tasting the best part of a French fry, especially if it's one covered in truffle oil?

It was easy for me to be my best self with Smooth, but not as easy to open up and talk about the not-so-great parts of me and my life. He thought that I had the perfect job (I didn't), I was making the perfect amount of money (I wasn't), and I had the perfect dog (that actually wasn't wrong). While it is incredibly important to want to be the best you can be for yourself and your partner, it's equally—if not more—important to be raw and real about things that aren't so great. Unfortunately, **vulnerability can be one of the hardest things to show in a relationship.**

The saddest thing was that Smooth always told me about his setbacks along with his wins. He was an open book with me. I, on the other hand, remained closed like Chik-fil-A on Sundays. The poor guy had no idea who I really was. Financially, I was spending every dollar I had to take us out on frivolous dates to impress him. He thought I had unlimited funds. Career-wise, I was unmotivated and struggling with a terrible boss. He thought I was enjoying traveling, working, and building an empire on the side. Emotionally, I was spending days depressed and working through an eating disorder. He thought I was happy and had no idea about my issues with food. In the end, I couldn't handle it anymore. My fear of being fully open and vulnerable ultimately led me to end the relationship—an end he definitely wasn't expecting. He was a victim of the crossfire between who I was and who I wanted to be. I broke Smooth's heart—a heart he had so openly and *vulnerably* given me.

Maybe if we had met later in life after I had faced the root of my woes, or at the very least, if I had talked to him honestly about hard things, our fate might have been different. But the truth is you should never play the "what if" game, especially when it comes to love because it keeps your mind—and therefore, you—stuck in the past and unable to move on. All too often we focus on what we could have done differently and play out alternative outcomes in our minds, instead of looking at things from an objective point of view, taking the lesson, and learning from it. When something ends, whether it is on good or bad terms, the best thing to do is to focus on what you can take away from the experience instead of dwelling on how things might have been. Ask yourself: What did I learn? How can I do better? It is only from a place of acceptance that we can begin to truly let go.

What is the lesson I learned from the ideal courtship I had with Smooth? The power of vulnerability. I struggled a hell of a lot with being vulnerable in most of my relationships. It was V. easy for me to talk about the good parts of myself; however, when it came time to talk about the nitty-gritty, not-so-amazing stuff, I would stall because I was scared I would lose the person. How ridiculous is *that?*

Picture this: you're in a healthy relationship with a wonderful person. They are respectful, kind, smart, loving, and all the good things you seek in a potential mate. What if you let nearly a year slip only showing them the good side of you when, well, your life was about to hit rock bottom? What if you were too scared to tell them the truth because you were afraid of how they would respond? If you weren't "perfect," then surely, they would pack up and leave, right? As someone who lived that story, I assure you, it's not a great feeling to be in a relationship with someone who has no idea there's a different side of you hiding in the other room.

What I *should* have been focused on was being raw and honest with him, sharing both my wins *and* my losses. If me being human (i.e., a person who makes mistakes) made him want to leave me, well, wouldn't that be a good thing? Who the hell wants to live a total lie? Nothing, no one, nada-freakin'-thing is absolutely perfect. You will never be too much for the right person.

Too often we fear that being vulnerable will lead to rejection or criticism. The fact is anyone who honestly cares for you will be glad you shared because it will allow you both to connect on a deeper level. **Vulnerability breeds true intimacy.** Isn't intimacy one of the many perks of being in a relationship? Of course, it's scary to put yourself out there. Vulnerability should only come when you trust someone, and they have shown you they are worthy enough to hear the things that aren't so easy for you to talk about.

Sometimes the scariest part of being vulnerable is admitting our own imperfections to *ourselves*. Self-reflection and realization can be brutal things to face but you cannot ignore your flaws forever. Your weak spots are just as much a part of you as your strengths. The thing is, no one is perfect. Wouldn't you rather be honest than go on living life through an Instagram filter? While I might look better to the masses with a flower crown and zero pores or wrinkles, it's *not* the real deal. How freakin' amazing does it feel when you're 100% yourself with someone—sharing even the bad stuff—and *that's* the reason they like you? I assure you, there is nothing better (except maybe sipping a perfectly spicy, skinny margarita while lying on a white sand beach).

Let's promise that no matter how fucking scary it is to put our fears, faults, and past out there in this big, bad world we live in, we're going to do the damn thing anyway. Glennon Doyle (aka the thought-provoking leader of the be-yourself-no-matter-what-and-own-it movement) reminds us that we *can* do hard things. I can't preach about how easy being vulnerable is and that everyone's going to accept you because, well, it's *not* easy and there *will* be people who won't accept you. I can promise though, that when you're speaking your truth, it feels really damn good. The question is: would you rather live life being loved as a masked version of yourself or live life being loved as your unapologetic and honest self? I'm gonna go ahead and keep my metaphorical mask off, knowing that I'm living *my* truth. What do you say: keep the mask on or take it off?

# Chapter 4—
# Spectacular Sex with a Hot Shot Comedian Should Be on Everyone's To-Do List

*Is sex dirty? Only when it's being done right.*
*—Woody Allen*

Throughout much of my dating life, I never felt totally feminine. A mere three chapters into this book I think I've made it clear that self-confidence has never been my strongest suit; but, beyond the "I don't think I'm good enough" inner mean-girl monologue, I never felt like much of a woman. I had no doubt that I identified as a woman, but femininity wasn't something I understood—especially when it came to the physical side of things. Let me put it this way: I would pray for a power outage when it came time for me to get naked in the presence of a good-looking man, simply because that would ensure no lights could be turned on.

Despite never feeling sexy, eventually I did feel somewhat comfortable with my body. I guess that just happens over time. I mean, you look at yourself naked every day for however many years, so you just kind of . . . get used to it. You can either accept it and decide to try to love it, change it, or hate yourself for the rest of eternity. In my case, when I least expected it, I met someone who was obsessed with my body, and I began to wonder what I hated all along. Let me be clear: who should dictate how awesome you are and how much you love your body? You! But I won't deny that it is V. nice to be around someone who appreciates what you've got going on!

If I ask you to describe the *best* sex of your life, what is the first thing that comes to mind? Is it with the love of your life on a balcony in the Mediterranean, a sexy new co-worker in the copy room, or a total stranger in an alley in Spain (probably not recommended but hey, you only live once and hopefully you used protection)? Where did it happen? Why was it so great? For me, the best sex of my life (before I met my husband who knocked the following experience right out of the water) happened in a rickety hotel room at the Stratosphere Casino in Las Vegas. The. Fucking. Stratosphere.

If you're not familiar with the Las Vegas Strip, the "Strat" is located at the V. northern tip and isn't exactly the typical Vegas hotel filled to the brim with high rollers, top chefs, and outrageously beautiful people. It's more like the seedy hotel on the corner that smells of stale cigarettes and exclusively hires cocktail waitresses in their sixties. *This* is the place where I have my bang of the decade? Why couldn't it have been at the Wynn or the Bellagio or, possibly, someone's home? Somewhere a little bit classier? That's the thing about sex: the location often has little to do with the level of heat between the sheets if there's insane chemistry involved.

I'm sure you're wondering about the dude, or at least what he looks like. Hey, physical attraction matters! I don't think *Fifty Shades of Grey* would have been such a hit if Mister-Grey-Will-See-You-Now wasn't super-hot, ultra-rich, and great in bed. So, who was the guy I had such incredible sex with? He was a comedian. A smokin' hot comedian who definitely had some things in common with Mr. Grey (minus the required contractual agreement). I didn't realize hot comedians who excel in the ~~bed~~ hotel room existed, but alas, here we are. He was enticing with tan skin, brown hair, blue eyes, and a great smile. And naturally, he was hilarious. Beyond being outrageously handsome and fun to talk to, *The Comedian* had one of the most beautiful penises I have ever seen in my entire life. Homeboy was rockin' a Grade A dick. Although I'm sure he wouldn't mind, I won't risk compromising this fellow's identity by going into further detail (because surely someone would look him up and slide into his DMs—and I wouldn't blame them).

The Comedian was obsessed with my body in the most flattering way. He liked everything, down to each (lack of) curve from my head to my toes. Everything I had always resented, he adored. And, best of all, he let me know how much he liked it. There is no better feeling than being naked with someone who compliments every square inch of you. Okay, well there are things that come close, like eating chips and guacamole while you bask in the sunlight of Cabo San Lucas; but the fact is, it feels pretty fucking awesome to have a super sexy person tell you that you are perfect just the way you are.

The point of this story is not in the details of the sexual experience; it is that I finally understood what I had been missing out on my entire life: in-fucking-credible sex! Why do we lower our standards and settle for anything other than spectacular—whether it be sex, a partner, a job, or our life? If you're anything like me (pre-comedian sex-capade), you might answer, "Well, Mikaela, because I live in the real world and that shit only exists in movies." I'm here to tell you it doesn't have to! As the girl who actually met her own living, breathing version of Mr. Grey, I can confirm that your real life (sex included) can be even *better* than what you see in a movie or read in a book.

The best part about my sexual encounter with The Comedian was that I discovered what I needed as far as sex was concerned. There is good sex, great sex, and mediocre sex. When you have mind-blowing, life-changing sex, you don't want anything less, like ever again. And why should you? You're awesome, remember? Awesome people deserve mind-blowing sex.

You know what else is awesome? *Communicating* what you like.

When you discover what you like and want as far as sex is concerned, it's V. important to ask for it (and ask for it often). And, if the person you are getting it on with is doing something you *don't* like, it's imperative to speak up. Sex is like a conversation; it's not pleasurable if it's distinctly one-sided. I remember feeling worried that if I spoke up about something that wasn't exactly doing the job, I'd ruin the mood or—worse—hurt my partner's feelings at a super intimate time. What could ruin the moment more than finding out you *didn't* rock your partner's world like they've never felt before?

Of course, there's a delicate way to communicate your wants, needs, likes, and dislikes in a way that won't derail the both of you from having an unforgettable roll in the hay. As we know, actions usually speak louder than words, so it might be worth a shot to demonstrate what you enjoy instead of trying to talk it through like you're reading bullet points from a PowerPoint presentation. Alternatively, you could say how much pleasure you get from "X" and see what happens from there. If someone told me they really liked something, I would more than likely go out of my way to make it happen for them. If they didn't like something, I wouldn't do it again. Most—if not all—of us want to please our partners in the bedroom (or wherever), but it's imperative we make sure *we're* taken care of as well. Spectacular sex is a delicate balance between being selfish and selfless.

Next time you're about to get freaky with Average Andrew or Boring Betty, remind yourself that you deserve metamorphic, cathartic, and transformative sex that makes you feel like you've levitated up into the clouds above you. Figure out what you like, what you need, and don't be afraid to ask for it. In fact, demand it! Repeat after me: **I am worthy of spectacular sex and will not waste my precious time on anything less.**

# Chapter 5—
# Pretending You're Katniss Everdeen When You're Really Blair Waldorf Is A V. Bad Idea

*Always be a first rate version of yourself and not a second rate version of someone else.*
*—Judy Garland*

I'm not sure what the deal was between me and nightclubs in my twenties, but apparently, I really did—on some level—believe I was Rihanna (don't worry, I have since come to my senses). One Halloween night I was in a mood, so I decided to skip dressing up in a costume and instead I hit my usual nightclub with one of my best friends at the time. Yes, we had a go-to nightclub—for no other reason than we got free drinks because her boyfriend was a bartender. We were huddled in a dark corner of the bar, ripping shots of tequila when I locked eyes with a caveman wearing tattered Vans who was *also* ripping shots of tequila. There's a reason Nicholas Sparks doesn't start his stories with multiple shots of tequila—it usually doesn't end well.

The caveman turned out to be *The German.* He swayed on over to me, introduced himself, and, well, I almost spat my tequila out on the poor guy because he had the same name as my dog. I have friends who won't date people with the same name as their brother, sister, or cousin, but dog? Why the hell not? It certainly made it easier for me to remember him the next morning when I woke up to a text from my dog (ahem, German caveman) telling me what a great time he had had the night before. To be honest, my recollection of the night was a little foggy, but I do remember there was a lot of dancing, ~~talking~~ screaming, and, you guessed it, tequila.

He asked me out on a date, and I decided it was worth a shot, mostly because I wasn't too sure what he even looked like (to be fair, he was wearing a wig and a costume that he *definitely* made himself five minutes before the Uber was set to arrive). The following Friday I found myself in a bowling alley with a handsome fellow who had his own engraved bowling ball. Listen, I am all about creative and unusual first dates, but bowling has never been my thing. First, putting on shoes that at least a thousand other people have worn—with or without socks—makes my inner germophobe shudder. Second, I'm terrible at the sport, and who likes being terrible at something on a first date?

Did I tell him how awful I was at bowling or that the thought of putting on rented shoes made me want to vomit? No! Instead, I exclaimed how much I *loved* bowling, how I couldn't believe that he had his *own* ball, and that bowling was one of my *favorite* things to do. Why did I pretend to like bowling? Because he was V. cute and V. nice, and I was worried that if I told him how I really felt, I would ruin the date.

The first date turned into a second date where we went bowling again (because he thought I liked it so much), and he bought me my own engraved ball! This then snowballed into me on an archery range early one Saturday morning. There I stood, like Katniss

Everdeen from *The Hunger Games*, with a bow and arrow I had purchased myself, screaming, "Check out that shot!" In reality, my ideal outdoor activity is hiking followed by relaxing at a spa with champagne or, better yet, lying on a yacht in the Mediterranean while a shirtless Chase Crawford serves me Dom Perignon a la *Gossip Girl*. I was pretending to be adventurous, archery badass Katniss, when honestly, I am more like five-star hotel-staying, champagne-loving Blair Waldorf.

This time, I had gone too far. I was pretending to be everything I wasn't just to impress a guy that, frankly, I wasn't compatible with (despite being wildly attracted to him). How many times have you pretended to like something just to impress someone you're interested in? I realize that most right-minded people wouldn't go so far as to purchase a bow and arrow at REI, but I bet we've all been guilty of pretending to be someone we're not for the sake of someone else, *especially* if it's a cute someone we have our eye on.

*Why* was I going to such lengths to impress him? The answer probably lies in the fact that, deep down, I knew our only connection was physical attraction, and I was grasping at any thread to keep the relationship going. It's great to be attracted to someone, but if you're looking for a serious relationship and there's nothing beyond a physical attraction, there isn't much point in continuing. It's a waste of time and energy for both of you. A bitter truth about time: you will never know how much of it you have left.

Here's another hard truth: when you're constantly pretending you love something you secretly can't stand, there will come a time when you cannot physically or mentally continue to be someone you're not. The truth *will* come out. In my case, it came out when

The German and I were having a nice dinner at his beachfront casita, and I suddenly blurted out "Can we go anywhere *but* the archery range?!" He looked at me like I had nineteen heads. He was understandably confused because he thought he had met his heroine soulmate who loved shooting bows and arrows on Saturday mornings. Needless to say, he was not my Peeta, and I was certainly not his Katniss.

It turns out that purchasing an expensive bow and arrow wasn't my ticket to epic love; this episode taught me that the way to impress a date isn't by pretending to like something they like. How do you *really* impress them? Do the thing they like when they know you don't like to do it or don't know much about it (and skip the complaining because that's never a good look). Why will that resonate? It will show that you're making an effort for them.

If you hate sports, don't secretly google what a red card means in soccer or order *Soccer for Dummies* on Amazon Prime One-Day. If the fact that you aren't into sports makes someone not want to date you, then let them ride off into the sunset to find a better match—someone who grew up with seventeen brothers and spends weekends playing flag football. Alternatively, this person might not mind that you aren't a big sports fan. If you show up on Sunday morning, homemade guacamole in hand, and ask a question every now and then, they'll probably be impressed that you made an effort to try to understand because they know it isn't your thing. If they're a keeper, they'll probably go out of their way to do something *they* don't like to do, but *you* do. In my case, the guy would agree to watch *The Notebook* with me. He might even actually like the movie because, ahem, most men I know secretly do. Similarly, you might find that soccer is a lot more enjoyable than you initially thought, or you might just feel good knowing that you made your partner happy.

I was so scared of losing The German because I didn't like bowling or archery (I, too, giggle when I read that ridiculous thought), but the truth is I had already lost because I wasn't being myself. Being vulnerable is one thing, but owning your likes and dislikes is pretty fucking important in a relationship too. Imagine if he and I had gotten married. Beside the fact that our wedding would probably take place in the middle of a forest with no bug spray in sight (aka my personal version of hell), can you imagine how miserable we would both be? Beyond being miserable, I would also be exhausted because it takes way more effort to be someone you're not than to just, you know, *be who you are*. Miserable and exhausted: two things you *shouldn't* be in a relationship.

What I should have been afraid of was losing *myself*. Why bend, morph, and become some unrealistic version of yourself to appear more attractive to whoever you're dating? Whether it's pretending to like sports, dressing in a certain way, reading pretentious books, or using certain language, why be anything other than your most authentic self? **The best relationships in our lives are the authentic ones.** You can't have an authentic relationship when you aren't being your *true* self.

Regardless of how attractive, charming, intelligent, and well-mannered your date is, if you can't be the *real* you around them, they're not the one for you. Of course, there is a time and a place for everything. If you have the mouth of a drunken sailor and "fuck" is your favorite four-letter word, you should rein it in when you're at church with your date and their parents. But, when you're raging with them at a live concert and your favorite song comes on, by all means, shout "Fuck yeah! I love this fucking song!" and pump your fist in the air like a groupie in the front row. Your person, your *Pride and Prejudice* kind of love, will love whatever it is that makes you, you.

Kurt Cobain said, "I'd rather be hated for who I am than loved for who I am not." As for me, I'd rather be loved by someone who knows the real me than loved by someone who doesn't know me at all. Being truly seen, flaws and all, dislikes, likes, and quirks, and loved *for those things* is much better than being adored by someone who thinks you love marathons when running from the couch to the fridge for a refill is your preferred physical activity.

When I started owning my authentic self—the passionate, quirky, sensitive me I had always kept hidden in previous relationships—there was a fuck ton of guys who didn't like it one bit. Did it sting, especially when they were seemingly amazing men? Of course it did! It's hard to be the real you and have someone say, "Yeah, I'm going to go ahead and pass." It can make you wonder if something is wrong with you. Honey, nothing is wrong with you, okay? If you feel like you need to dull your sparkle and hide your real self for someone, it's a clear indicator they aren't your forever person. The unpleasant reality you must accept is that there are going to be people who don't like you. The trick is finding the person that does. Don't go through life trying to win an Oscar for your performance in the film, *Pretending to Be Someone I'm Not (A Memoir).*

# Chapter 6—
# You Probably Shouldn't Fly Across the Country to Have Sex with Someone You've Never Met

*Maybe it did take a crisis to get to know yourself; maybe you needed to get whacked hard by life before you understood what you wanted out of it.*
*—Jodi Picoult*

If you were to write a book about your past dating life, there would probably be at least one chapter you'd hope your mother would never read. As a warning, mom, this is *that* chapter (and yes, I realize I've already written about someone's Grade A dick).

Raise your hand if you've ever felt personally victimized by your own choices in your dating life. Yours truly has had a number of what-the-fuck-was-I-thinking moments ranging from going out on a date with a married man (there's a future chapter about that dumpster fire) to leaving someone mid-first date pretending I needed to use the bathroom and subsequently running out the door like I had just shit my pants. Flying three thousand miles to spend a weekend with a guy I had never met trumps them all.

I met the guy, who I like to call *Mr. East Coast*, in the most romantic way. Just kidding—we matched on Tinder while he was on vacation in Las Vegas. Unfortunately, he was flying back home the next day. East Coast was the epitome of charm, and unbeknownst to me at the time, a complete fuckboy. He was highly intelligent, direct, and quite frankly, didn't give two shits about my heart. What does an insecure woman who is getting over a messy breakup love more than a bottomless mimosa brunch on Sunday? In this case, a guy that doesn't care all that much about her or her heart. I was:

a) attaching myself to a clearly bad scenario
and
b) ignoring every gut feeling I had.

If you've ever fallen for someone who didn't reciprocate the emotion, you might understand this situation.

It's a tale as old as time: the person you like doesn't like you back. They are, like the book and the movie, just not that into you. For some reason, you decide to ignore this and continue trying because everyone changes their mind after the fifteenth try (unfortunately, they almost always don't).

East Coast was *just* nice enough to keep me around. He was a high school P.E. teacher, a devoted uncle to two adorable, young girls, and had a master's degree. Stable job? Check. Good with kids? Check. Intelligence, and an intriguing personality? Check. And then he sent me a shirtless photo. *Checkmate.* Thankfully, the unsolicited photo was not a dick pic. It was a shirtless selfie in the mirror at his beach house. I've read too many romance novels not to see if this beach house was part of my sought-after Hallmark Channel ending.

East Coast called, texted, and/or FaceTimed me daily. It got to the point where I expected to talk to him—even though we had never met in person. One evening he casually asked, "Have you ever been to the Northeast?" and I had a flight booked five days later (paid for by none other than East Coast himself). The texts and the calls continued until the fated weekend arrived. I have no idea what I expected out of that weekend, or why I flew three thousand miles to see someone I barely knew. But I had already had a few V. spontaneous "screw it" moments, so this had to join the list. There is no greater "screw it" moment than when you're stepping off a plane and are about to meet (and have sex with) a guy you have never met in person before. We've all had experiences we're not too proud of—this is one of mine.

It was *not* a Hallmark worthy greeting. He didn't even meet me at the airport. He wasn't waiting for me with a handwritten sign and freshly picked flowers. Instead, I had to navigate an airport I'd never been to before, call an Uber, and meet East Coast in an Uno's Pizzeria parking lot in the middle of a snowstorm. I was out of breath and wondering how to function in sub-seventy-degree weather, and at the same time blown away by how attracted I was to him in real life. I remember looking over at him, after a quick hello, and thinking to myself, "Holy shit, this guy is way hotter in person." It was an effortless kind of hot, but I'm sure he knew how good-looking he was. He also got me a nice-to-finally-meet-you present, which consisted of a card, chocolate, tequila, and red wine. Who's to say this guy didn't know the way to my heart? JK, he totally got lucky.

I caught feelings for my cross-country Tinder date after spending most of that long weekend alone with him in a car, driving.

While it might sound implausible to fall for someone in a weekend (unless you're a contestant on *The Bachelor*), there is no riskier situation than being in the ultimate romantic movie moment: driving tree-lined, snowy highways and New England back roads; getting to know each other; and exchanging the most personal of stories. It was the perfect disaster. I was caught off guard, and I let my heart take the wheel when I really should have let my brain keep driving. My heart was squealing, "OMG, this is so romantic! We're running together on the beach with his dogs, eating at fabulous restaurants, and fucking in a beach house!" while my brain was screaming, "Hold it right there sista! Back to reality! This guy is not looking for anything serious!" So, did I ignore my mind or my heart?

I let the gorgeous scenery and the dreamy idea of it all take over my common sense and ignored who was standing right in front of me: a guy just looking for a good time. Matters got worse when our extended weekend came to an end and East Coast let it slip that he had caught feelings for me too. Did I hold on to that as if my (love) life depended on it? Absolutely. On my flight home, I felt blindsided: how can someone make such an impact on your life in such a short amount of time and, more importantly, how can you let them?

Our conversations didn't end after that weekend when, perhaps, they should have. The calls and texts continued, and another trip was planned. The California girl returned to the Northeast a month later. I should mention that month apart seemed devastatingly long, at least for me. Unfortunately, one month is plenty of time for your heart to trick your brain into thinking something it shouldn't. It went a little something like this:

Heart: "Isn't it so romantic East Coast reaches out to me every day? We are spending another weekend together (well, just a day, but that's okay!) in a month. Because he talks to me every day, I know he likes me as much as I like him."

Brain: "Are you sure? I don't think so . . . I think he just likes having sex and doing fun things . . .?"

Heart: "Nooooo, it's way more than just sex."

Brain: ". . . ok . . ."

Newsflash: it was obviously about sex.

The weekend I had longed for came, and it was at the same time one of the best and worst weekends of my life. Seeing East Coast was like having energy in my soul because he was invigorating, sexy, and different from anyone I had been with before. And I was on vacation—who doesn't enjoy hot sex with a hot human when they're on vacation? We had a magical night: there was live music and lots of drinking, handholding, dancing, and sex—lots of sex. Then, just like that, it was over. He was gone before 9 a.m. with nothing more than a quick goodbye containing a *microscopic* ounce of emotion. Seriously, he didn't even give me a hug before his departure.

To go from such a feverish high to a crashing low in a matter of twenty-four hours is a disorienting feeling—one that makes you ask yourself, "How the hell did I get here?" After what seemed like the longest flight home I have ever endured, filled with nothing but regrets and questions, I laid in bed berating myself for putting myself in this situation—I had lost myself for the sake of attention from someone else. Finally, I decided to listen to my brain. I realized that

I was in a fucked-up situation that I could have easily avoided and acknowledged that he was just not that into me. My heart was broken, and the damage was done. Emotions: sometimes the heaviest ones hit you all at once.

Things got worse on the Monday after I got home. We exchanged what would become the final texts of our faux-lationship. It wasn't a good interaction. It went something like: "I like you and had a good weekend. I'd like to see where things go." to which he responded (I'm paraphrasing) "I'm sorry. I am a realistic dude with a cold soul and wouldn't mind if we never saw each other again."

After that doozy of a conversation, we didn't talk again. Shocking, I know. When you've talked to someone daily for months and then the communication suddenly cuts off, it's jarring. I was upset so I blocked him on every social media outlet and deleted his number and all evidence of his existence from my phone. Someone can be a part of your life, and with the click of a few buttons, it can be like they never existed in the first place. Except they *did* exist and, unfortunately for anyone who has ever suffered heartbreak, we don't have that same delete button for our minds.

Upset, angry, confused, and rejected were just a few of the words that could have described my emotional state. My initial reaction, likely spurred by my inability to hold myself accountable, along with my friends building me up and texting me "Screw that guy!", was to blame him. How could he do this? How could he text me every day, talk to me, learn about me, tell me about himself, fly me to his side of the country with absolutely zero intention of a serious relationship? How could he let this happen? What an asshole!

I have to acknowledge that, while he could have been more forthcoming about his emotional unavailability and his text was V. much an asshole move, he never forced me to do anything. He didn't force me to fly there, to talk to him every day, and most importantly, to let him in my heart (and my pants). Those were all *my* decisions. In short, this one was on me. After I came to this realization, the next set of emotions included wallowing in my own guilt and self-loathing. I punished myself for being such a fool. I went the full twelve rounds with my thoughts, and I was bloody and ready to pass out in the corner. It wasn't pretty; but, despite the epic mistake, I should have offered myself a little more grace.

We're in this crazy thing called life with no direction whatsoever. Sure, there are some standard guidelines for what to do versus what not to do (you heard it here first: don't fly to Boston to meet a guy you matched with on Tinder), but really, there is a lot of trial and error. You win some, and you lose some. In the world of dating, we have all had times when we were the victors, and other times when we were the victims (unless you're Priyanka Chopra, because it seems like she's always victorious). Are you going to be the victim who breaks down, cries, wallows in pain, and never moves on? Or are you going to be the kind of person who feels all the feels, then looks at what happened and decides to push forward even though it still stings?

Just because I made a mistake, I didn't have to kick myself in the ass every day. What I needed to do was to learn to do better and have a little bit (a lot) more self-control and some motherfucking self-respect. We all make mistakes. Mistakes are valuable because they (hopefully) teach us lessons. This is how we grow and learn. **Mistakes can lead to breakthroughs, and pain can lead to purpose.** This is what I learned from my most memorable what-the-fuck-was-I-thinking moment:

a) The Northeast is beautiful. Go visit.
b) Trust your heart, but don't stop listening to your mind.
c) Behind every rejection is a redirection.

I needed to be redirected; I needed to have something happen (in this case, rejection from an East Coast fuckboy) to help me change the trajectory of my life and, ultimately, re-discover *myself.* Oh yes, the P.E. teacher from the Northeast is the guy behind the meltdown referenced in the beginning of this book. His rejection spurred me on to the expedition that not only helped me finally heal some serious trauma wounds, but also freed me from the cycle of attracting fuckboy after fuckboy. Ultimately, I learned to love the fuck out of the person I saw in the mirror. The pain his rejection caused led me straight into my purpose. So, thanks East Coast . . . I guess.

When we think of something as meant to be, we automatically assume forever. But maybe it doesn't always have to be forever. Maybe someone or something enters your life to teach you a lesson (or two). Are you going to try to understand the lesson at hand, or ignore it and move on to the next person behind door number two? If you refuse to feel your emotions (even the terrible ones), they don't just disappear. In my experience, the same fuckboy (with a different face each time) showed up over and over until I finally understood, learned the damn lesson, and got the breakthrough I needed. Maybe the forever part isn't the *person*, but what we *gain* from our relationship (or faux-lationship) with them. What can you learn from your latest what-the-fuck moment, and, most importantly, what are you going to do about it?

# Chapter 7— Get Out of Your Comfort Zone: A Tropical Rendezvous with a Cruise Ship Musician

*Real change is difficult at the beginning, but gorgeous at the end. Change begins the moment you get the courage and step outside your comfort zone; change begins at the end of your comfort zone.*
*—Roy T. Bennett*

There's nothing better than going on a vacation, am I right? Although, I'm sure we can collectively agree that *some* vacations are better than others (cough, my quick weekends in New England, cough). Personally, I thought trips during my twenties would be spent with my soulmate, frolicking on the Amalfi coast, sipping something perfectly chilled and certainly alcoholic, and eating pasta without gaining a pound. Unfortunately, my twenties were less *Eat, Pray, Love* and more *National Lampoon's Vacation*. I spent one of the most notable holidays of my early twenties on a Caribbean cruise with my parents. In case you're wondering, we three amigos shared a room. Nothing says, "I'm independent!" like splitting a 100-square-foot cabin with your parents on a cruise ship. I realize I *should* have been uber grateful to be privileged enough to go on a vacation and spend precious time with my aging parents, but I was going through some serious mental shit at the time and couldn't appreciate waking up in the morning, let alone traveling the crystal blue waters with good ole mom and dad.

Luckily, on the very first day my attitude changed when I, boy-crazy Mikaela, you guessed it, met a boy. I locked eyes with *The Sexy Saxophonist* (they do exist) during the opening night of the cruise's musical productions. I was in the third row, pouting about sitting with my parents instead of a hunky boyfriend or some girlfriends (ungrateful much?), when the lights dimmed, the curtains pulled back, and I saw the most beautiful mocha-latte-of-a-musician. He had a solo, and it felt like it was just me and him with the smoothest of smooth jazz playing in the background. *Titanic* had nothing on our love story. At the end, he winked in my direction, and I looked behind me, certain that this flirtatious gesture was meant for someone else. Unless homeboy was into eighty-five-year-old married women holding hands with their husbands, he was definitely winking at me. Again with the eye contact!

I walked back to our stateroom, tipsy mom and dad in tow, wondering what the hell I should do. *I mean, I was on vacation with my frickin' parents,* and I didn't feel like I had any accolades that would attract a cruise ship musician. While I'm aware that cruise ship musician isn't exactly equivalent to POTUS or even CEO, my self-worth was at an all-time low. It made me uncomfortable just thinking about it. How would I approach him? What would I say? How could we even hang out? What would the point of hanging out be?

I was stressing out about talking to a cute boy on a cruise ship in one of the most beautiful places in the world. Talk about first world problems. The next morning, I was running on the treadmill, staring out into the vast sea of blue in front of me, and who should hop on the treadmill to my right? The Sexy Saxophonist! We must have hit a big wave, or I was totally caught off guard (this is the real reason), because I stumbled and almost flew off my damn machine. The Universe works in mysterious ways, my darling, especially when it sends you a tall, handsome saxophonist on a cruise ship who makes you so nervous you trip on a treadmill headed for St. Thomas. Despite all my worries and apprehension, I decided to throw caution to the wind. I said hello, made a bad joke about my V. ungraceful fall, and waited to see what the hell happened next.

What happened? Only the most amazing ten days with a beautiful, talented, and well-traveled man. He took me to all the non-touristy places I never would have visited otherwise, like a redneck bar in the Caribbean, a hotel tucked away in the middle of nowhere with the most beautiful pool you could ever imagine, and a beach where you can buy bottles of rum and drink openly for every beachgoer to see. We had a blast. Well, we had a blast *off* the ship, because it's an epically huge no-no for employees to fraternize with guests. But fraternize we did and, oh man, what fun we did have (I'm happy slash shocked to report that I didn't get it on with him. Yay me!).

Our fun together was short lived because it was an eleven-day itinerary and, you know, you can't exactly stay on a cruise ship for free. I got caught up in the situation and remember being so torn up about it, wondering if I'd ever see him again as if I were Harper from *Ibiza: Love Drunk* leaving Leo West after their wild Spanish rendezvous. I did see The Sexy Saxophonist again although nothing ever came of it. He's living his best life on the other side of the country and continues to hold the title of the sexiest ~~saxophonist~~ musician I've ever met. Well, I guess it's a toss-up between him and Smooth.

It wasn't until many years later that I realized the whole point of my short-lived adventure with him wasn't to fall in love, but to help me get out of my own head. It forced me to step out of my comfort zone. At the time, I was reeling from two really bad experiences that left me questioning just about every man I met. We'll get to what exactly happened in the next section, but the point is, I was stuck. I was in a black hole of depression, uncertainty, shame, and guilt. The Universe gave me exactly what I needed when I needed it: a reprieve from everything I was struggling with internally. Unfortunately, the Universe doesn't always send us a gift in the form of a ruggedly handsome saxophonist, but I got lucky. Thanks, Universe.

Have you ever been so stuck in your head, ruminating on everything that has gone wrong, that you can't enjoy anything around you, even if it's something so lovely as a Caribbean cruise with your parents in the middle of January? Well, that was me. Hopeless. Hating men. Hating life. Even though all signs were pointing to, ummm, girlfriend you are, like, *really* freaking lucky.

I needed a jolt, a push, a sign that calmer waters were ahead (pun intended). And the Universe gave me what I needed. Think back on your life—the good moments, the bad moments, and the what-the-fuck moments. I'm absolutely positive the Universe sent you *exactly* what you needed *exactly* when you needed it. It could have been a lesson, a desire come to fruition, a saxophonist, or a fuckboy from the Northeast who broke your heart, but the Universe always has your back. Sometimes it's easy to recognize this fact, while at other times you're kind of like, "Huh?" I guarantee though, that when you look back, you can always connect the dots—even for the super-fucking-terrible stuff. There is always a reason and a *purpose*. Most of the time, we can't understand this when we're in the midst of whatever it is we're going through.

What was the purpose of my unexpected Caribbean semi-lover? He showed me the importance of getting out of my comfort zone, which at that time involved keeping my nose in a book or watching TV alone to escape my reality. It certainly wasn't enjoying the sights, sounds, and smells of my beautiful surroundings, or saying hello to a sexy saxophonist who just watched me almost fall off a treadmill.

Can you imagine if I never said hi? If I never convinced him that I could keep a secret like a CIA agent? If I never frolicked in the bluest water, semi-buzzed on the most delicious rum drink you could ever imagine, next to a man who could have been a model but decided he wanted to play saxophone in the middle of the ocean instead? Well, I would have missed out on all those amazing experiences because I was too scared, stuck, or unsure to try. And, of course, I wouldn't be writing this chapter trying to convince you to get the heck out of your comfort zone and put yourself out there. Hun, **life is too damn short to be afraid of making the first move.** Why not ask that cutie out? Don't be afraid to tell someone how you feel because you're worried they won't feel the same.

I can't promise you're going to experience success every time you leap into the giant abyss of the unknown, but I can guarantee that you will at least have a *chance* at success. Do you want to play small, be the same person you were yesterday, and never take any chances for the rest of your life? Assuming the answer to that is no, you have got to play big every now and again. You've got to take risks, crawl out of your comfortable hole, and do things that feel unnatural and scary AF. You must try this because it is the only way you're going to have new experiences and grow as a human.

I'll be the first one to admit that taking a risk and putting yourself out there is really fucking uncomfortable. I'm sure you're thinking, "Okay, Mikaela, but frolicking around drunk in the Caribbean with a hot guy doesn't sound remotely uncomfortable." And yes—you're right! But what if I told you that a year prior, I had fallen victim to something really fucking terrible with a hot guy? It was so hard for me to get the courage up to just say hi to The Saxophonist. Trusting people again after being epically hurt is uncomfortable. But **we have got to get comfortable with being uncomfortable—the ability to fall in epic love with our lives depends on it.**

The cool thing about stepping out of your comfort zone is that everyone's zone is different. What's difficult for me might be easy for my BFF, and vice versa. Why is that cool? Because we have people who can help us when we're about to turn around, play it safe, and remain in Comfort-ville. They can support us when the fear of uncertainty is too big to face alone.

While friends or family can offer you support when you need it, there's something infinitely more powerful that's willing to offer you aid, courage, or comfort whenever you ask for guidance or help when things become a little too uncomfortable. The Universe wants you to dream big and take risks that might feel scary AF—it also knows that you are totally capable of doing the damn thing anyway.

So, what do you say? Are you ready to make the first move and leave the safe (boring) harbor behind? You are the captain of your cruise ship. You have a compass deep within you that won't lead you astray. It's time to say hi to the sexy saxophonist waiting to ride the waves with you.

# Part II
# Acknowledgement

*(from an Overwhelmed Gal Chugging Rosé Because She Can't Believe She Kept Doing the Same Things but Expected a Different Outcome—#INSANITY)*

# Chapter 8—
# You Can't Break Up with Your Past

*We are products of our past, but we don't have to be prisoners of it.*
*—Rick Warren*

I'm going to challenge you to do something that is V. crucial to changing your (dating) life for good. Seriously, if you skip this incredibly difficult, totally uncomfortable step in the process, there's a good chance you might find yourself repeating similar versions of my mistakes. Do you want to keep doing dumb shit, like having sex with someone who doesn't know (or care to find out) your middle name? I'm going to assume the answer is no, since you bought a book about falling in epic love. What's the next step, might you ask?

It's time to acknowledge what the fuck has happened. It's time to start to connect the dots, observe any patterns, find the root of the issue, and address it. It's time to face the music about your mistakes and, more importantly, what is causing them. This is the hardest part because you have to think about all the things you probably *don't* want to think about. You have to address parts of yourself that you might not be proud of or recall experiences that might not have been enjoyable. I went there and I came out on the other side—so I believe in my heart that you can too. Please know that while my experiences might not be identical to yours, the way to heal is the same: by facing the things you don't want to face, accepting them, and acknowledging their effects. **It's only by becoming aware of what the hell is going on that you can start to change.**

When I was a child, my family would spend most holidays with my dad's relatives. Whether it was out of familial obligation or convenience (they lived five minutes away), every Thanksgiving, Christmas Eve, and New Year's Day was held at my dad's parents' house. And I fucking hated it. My parents, my brother, and I would walk in the door, and, like clockwork, I became invisible. Everyone else would be having a great time cooking, chatting, and being together while I'd usually sit in a chair in the corner by myself or go upstairs and play on the computer alone. I remember feeling like I didn't matter, like my cousins and even my older brother were more liked than me—it was always evident, but I remember feeling it most on Christmas Eve.

Without fail, the large tree would be exploding with presents. Seriously, there had to be hundreds of boxes—they would almost fill up the dining room. They were meticulously wrapped, as my dad's mother was not only always sharply dressed, but also had an eye for design. She could have been Meryl Streep's character Miranda Priestly in *The Devil Wears Prada*—I can't watch that movie without thinking of her. Of course, as a child, I loved presents. After dinner, the time finally came to open the gifts—the time all the kids had been waiting 364 days for. It was usually my job, along with the next youngest cousin, to divvy up the presents for each of the recipients. Everyone took a chair, and we would rush to place the gifts at each family member's spot. And every year, I wondered why my pile wasn't as big as my cousins', and why my grandmother couldn't spell my name correctly. I questioned what was wrong with me, in what ways I wasn't good enough, and why nobody in my family seemed to notice, let alone care.

I'll never forget the year when I opened my gift to find perfume samples—you know, the samples you get for free at the counter at Macy's. I tried to hold back tears as my cousin got a very expensive gift, screamed in glee, and hugged our grandmother with all her might. I couldn't help but wonder, "What did I do wrong? Why doesn't she love me? Why doesn't she . . . like me?" Presents aren't the point of Christmas, and the smaller pile or less expensive gift isn't what made me sad. It was the seemingly intentional difference in how I was treated compared to everyone else that made me feel like an outcast in my own family—the family I had been taught would love me more than anyone else in the world. It got to the point where, struggling with debilitating anxiety, I would cry myself to sleep the night before the holidays and spend the night after in sheer emotional pain. I tried to talk to my mother about it, but she wasn't much help. My grandmother didn't seem to like her all that much either. And my dad didn't understand what was happening until it was much too late.

While my relationship with my grandmother was difficult, the hardest part about the holidays—the part I dreaded—was having to spend time with my grandfather. When I was playing upstairs on the computer, he would always come in to "help" me—and by help, I mean touch me in the most inappropriate way. I was far too young to understand what the touching was. Even now, my brain doesn't allow me to fully remember when it started or when it ended, and I only have fuzzy memories of moments in the computer room on the second level. Six-year-old me became twenty-something-year-old me: a confused and broken soul still wondering what the hell was so wrong with her. I carried this shameful secret with me for so long—a secret I couldn't bear to tell the one person who probably needed to know: my dad. My lifelong secret obviously affected me in a multitude of ways, but the overwhelming effect on my self-worth became evident as I grew from a young girl into a young woman. While I had physically grown up, mentally I was, in many ways, the same solemn girl who believed that everyone else was better than she could ever be.

Victims of child abuse face a lifetime of psychological and physical effects that differ from person to person. In my experience, the effects manifested as extremely low self-esteem and difficulty in my relationships—both romantic and platonic—as well as unhealthy sexual practices. (Mr. East Coast ring a bell?) Looking back, I wish I had been strong enough to speak up and talk about what happened. I didn't have a place where I felt safe enough to do that, so I suffered silently until I became an adult and told my dad I would no longer be attending gatherings with his family. I know I hurt him deeply with my choice—especially because he didn't know the entire story. Unfortunately, my decision fractured his relationship with his parents—and it never mended. I know it haunts him to this day as they have since passed away. I remind myself often that my guilt is unwarranted, and I did what was best for me and my mental health.

Often, the most painful memories are the most difficult to

remember. Our minds are complex and skilled at covering up moments from our past to protect us from a harrowing reality. For most of my life, I kept a secret to protect my loved ones. What I didn't realize was that my efforts to protect everyone else left me very much unprotected—unprotected from shame, anger, and dysfunction. Bearing this secret kept me stuck in the mindset of the same six-year-old girl who, all those years ago, felt confused, hurt, and not worthy of anything remotely good.

While my story may not look like yours, it's important to connect with your inner child who may not have been heard and acknowledge the past. This can be one of the most difficult things to do, especially if you must recognize something that is painful; but when you become aware of something traumatic and acknowledge its effects, that is when the true healing can begin. While reflecting on my past, I started to see a pattern of feeling and behavior: low self-worth and unhealthy sexual practices. After identifying this pattern, it was important for me to find the source of it, and acknowledge it head on. Acknowledging what happened doesn't mean that it was okay. It is simply admitting that it did, in fact, happen. Just because I am now at peace with what happened does not mean I am without pain when I reminisce. To this day, Christmas remains my least favorite day of the year—and I am okay with that. I no longer feel like a prisoner of my past, I just accept that it is a part of who I am.

After I acknowledged the deep-seated root of my problems, I then had to work through and heal from it. This was no easy task. We all experience a wide variety of things, and our journey to healing can look a million different ways. Sometimes it takes longer than we would like. Healing isn't easy for people who are mentally or emotionally weary; remember that you do have the power to heal and change. You aren't changing because you're a broken person or a bad person, you're simply changing habits that aren't serving you and the epic love and life you deserve.

The path to true healing begins and ends with you—and it begins with acknowledging the root. Just like you can't break up with yourself, you also can't break up with your past.

# Chapter 9—
# A V. Bad Case of Hawaiian PTSD

*There are wounds that never show on the body that are deeper and more hurtful than anything that bleeds.*
*—Laurell K. Hamilton*

When I was seventeen, I somehow convinced my usually strict parents to let me spend my final high school summer in Hawaii working as a nanny for my Jamba Juice manager's children. "No big deal" I thought, as I hopped on the plane, excited for my extended Hawaiian vacation. Like most teenagers, I had no care or fear in the world and was totally unaware of the impending event that would change my life.

The summer went by quickly, as summers unfortunately always do. By the end of my eight-ish weeks in paradise, not only was I rocking an amazing tan (this was before I realized how much I hate the sun—SPF is now my BFF), but I also had formed a few friendships, and not-so-shockingly, met a cute surfer boy along the way. Said cute surfer boy was a couple of years my senior—I probably didn't make it too obvious that I wasn't even of age. Oh, to be young and naive again. (These days I'm legitimately overwhelmed with happiness if a waiter cards me at dinner.) I'd go out and meet him at the occasional party, maybe have a cocktail or two, share a kiss, and then be on my merry way back to the house where I was staying. This was a regular occurrence that felt almost normal by the inevitable time I had to go back to the mainland.

It was on the very last night that lovestruck me lost her virginity to *The Hawaiian.* Unfortunately for me, I had no idea I had had sex for the first time until I woke up in a strange place, naked in another person's bed. I groggily sat up and wondered what the hell was going on. Two minutes ago, I had been playing Monopoly (this is by no means an exaggeration—we were playing a board game). What the fuck happened? For starters, enthusiastic consent from both parties—especially not a V. unconscious me—did *not* happen.

Reality hit me in the face when I slowly got out of the bed, saw blood stains on the sheets, and felt an unfamiliar ache between my legs. I came to the shocking realization I was no longer a virgin and had had no say in the matter. In short, The Hawaiian put something in my drink and took my virginity when I was drugged and totally incoherent. For years, the hopeless romantic side of me had dreamed of the night I would become a woman—certain it would be with the man of my dreams who loved me more than anything. Unfortunately, that was not the case. To say I was forever changed would be a wild understatement. My attitude on the flight back home was certainly not as carefree as the flight months prior. Once again, I was bearing a secret I would keep with me (and me alone) for years to come. I was ashamed to tell anyone what happened because I felt like it was my fault. During the following year, most of my friends were frolicking about, enjoying the final year of high school as seniors normally do. On the outside, I tried to be the same me, but on the inside I silently suffered. *Everything* about me had changed. Love was no longer an idyllic, unwavering fairy tale—love became sex, and both became synonymous with pain.

A year later, during my first semester away at college, I found myself at a party held by one of the most popular fraternities on campus. Why? Because, well, that's where most of my fellow college freshman friends went as part of their nightly routine, and my teenaged self was simply trying to fit in. Unfortunately, I fell victim again. This time it was at the hands of a horrible *Freshman Fuckboy* who assaulted me in the bathroom, walked out, and lied to everyone about it when, this time, I tried to tell the truth. The truth fell on deaf ears because of a system that wasn't set up to support the victim. How could this have happened to me again? What had I done to deserve this fate? While I knew I'd never be able to escape the fact that these terrible things happened to me, it took me many years to fully realize the effect they were having on my relationships, and in particular, my romantic ones. Just about everything I acknowledged I was doing in my relationships (and faux-lationships) had a direct relationship to being abused and raped years prior. My relationship problems following these tragic incidents further justified my belief that love was a ruthless combination of sex and pain, and I needed external validation and acceptance to feel remotely okay.

Trauma is a very real, very serious, and, unfortunately, very common thing. NAMI (The National Alliance on Mental Illness) reports that over half of the adult population experience a traumatic event at least once in their lifetime. When I think about that statistic, I cannot believe that I spent years feeling completely alone (metaphorically speaking, because clearly I spent a whole lot of time with a whole lot of fuckboys who didn't care about my heart). **Please know, if you have experienced something traumatic, that you are *not* and never will be alone.** If you were the victim of something, it was *not* and never will be your fault. And, most importantly, you have all the power within you to heal from whatever happened.

So, what the hell is trauma and how does one go about healing from it? Trauma is any event that disrupts your sense of control and reduces your ability to connect current circumstances to reality. It's something that is too much, too soon. When most people hear the word "trauma", they think about Big T Trauma—war, rape, abuse, and other wildly catastrophic events. Big T Trauma is an extraordinary occurrence that leaves the victim feeling powerless and helpless. I was powerless and helpless at the hands of the two men who raped me and the man who abused me as a young girl. I had no control over these events just like someone who is in a plane crash has zero control over what is happening. For most trauma survivors, it takes a lot of time (and therapy) to feel like they're truly in control again.

What's seldom talked about is small t trauma. By this I mean other events that disrupt your sense of control—things that cause an interruption in your emotional regulation. Maybe a teacher told you how dumb you were when you were seven; maybe your parents got divorced; maybe your boyfriend cheated on you—this is all trauma. Regardless of how big or small it seems to you or someone else, *any* kind of trauma can have an effect on you.

Depending on the circumstance, you may develop post-traumatic stress disorder, or PTSD. Your values, morals, past experiences, beliefs, and level of distress tolerance are all factors that play into your predisposition to PTSD. I had placed an enormous value on losing my virginity and had a clear picture of how I wanted it to happen. Because that was taken away from me in the most horrific way, it's no wonder I was so deeply affected. My reaction is not a reflection of the strength of my psyche, mind you, and the same goes for anyone else. I avoided dealing with how I was feeling so I could appear strong and tough to everyone else. Little did I realize that avoiding my trauma was only exacerbating the problem.

Thankfully, there are many resources available for trauma survivors. The University of Pittsburgh Medical Center breaks the treatment process into three stages. The first stage focuses on safety and stabilization, which helps you learn how to regulate your emotions and feel safe again. In my own experience, Mindfulness Based Stress Reduction (MBSR) and somatic therapy were extremely helpful in achieving those goals. In the second phase, you concentrate on remembering the event and mourning what occurred, with an ultimate goal of being able to talk about what happened to you with no emotions attached (you aren't re-living it). Regular talk therapy is helpful here, although maintaining somatic therapy and MBSR can be important to help you feel safe. The third phase centers on reconnection and integration—honoring that this is a story in your life, but it is *not* the story that defines you. Many people find that giving back to communities and helping others by discussing their story empowers their own healing and recovery process. A part of my own healing journey is this very book, which I hope helps anyone who suffered like me.

Before I got help, I didn't realize how PTSD was influencing my romantic relationships with ~~men~~ fuckboys. By holding on to these horrific incidents, I was unknowingly holding myself back not only from truly healing, but also from experiencing what I truly wanted: an amazing, secure, and epic real-lationship. Over a decade later I was acting as if these past traumatic events were Steven Spielberg and my love life was the newest movie to hit the silver screen. My Trauma was calling the shots, and the skewed definition of love it created was guiding me to make all the wrong choices.

One of the biggest struggles I faced was feeling like it was *my* fault. In my mind, it had to be because it happened more than once. I kept replaying the scenes in my head, chastising myself for going to that fraternity party when I really should have been studying for Economics, or having that drink in Hawaii when I should have had water. If I had just done something differently, it never would have happened. The "what if" game I was playing had to stop. There are a multitude of scenarios, but the reality is what happened, *happened.* It never was nor will it ever (in a million Universes) be my fault. The only way I could hold myself accountable would be if I had a crystal ball, knew exactly what was going to happen, and put myself in those awful situations anyway. The last time I checked, life-predicting crystal balls weren't on sale at Target. I needed to accept that **it was not my fault.**

If something happened to you, it was not and never will be your fault; but, the ball *is* in your court to address what happened, work through all of the emotions, and heal from it so it doesn't continue to affect you and your life for the rest of, you know, your life. Beyond therapy, there are other wonderful tools to offer additional support throughout your healing process: reading, journaling, meditating, screaming into your pillow for fifteen minutes—whatever it is that you find helpful, let it help you face it head on. There is no other way to come out on the other side.

Acknowledging what happened instead of avoiding the issue is step number one. Why do we want to avoid it? Well, because acknowledging it likely brings back all the not-so-great feelings and emotions, and we have to admit that this *thing* happened to us. Who wants to feel epically crappy and recognize something bad happened to you? I don't blame you if you aren't raising your hand because neither did I, but the reality is this will affect you for the rest of your life *until you deal with it.* IDK about you, but I wanted my life back, and I was really tired of fucking around with fuckboys who loved playing games with my heart for the sake of a roll in the hay.

My self-worth was shattered because of the traumas I suffered; I felt tarnished and like I wasn't worthy of a decent relationship. I was acting like I was trash because some assholes decided to take advantage of me in the worst kind of way. If anything, those men were the human equivalent of garbage for doing what they did. The fact I fell victim to them had nothing to do with whether I deserved a great relationship. My ability to survive and be resilient enough to move on with my life shows what a strong, badass woman I am. Strong, badass people are ab-so-fuck-ing-lute-ly worthy of incredible, epic love. It's basically science. You are a resilient badass too, and you most certainly are worthy of the most wonderful kind of love.

I wish there were a cure for trauma and PTSD, but unfortunately, there's no magic pill. If one existed, you can bet your bottom dollar I would have sold every single thing I owned, took out a loan if I needed more money, run without shoes to the store that sold it, and waited hours overnight in line with no jacket in the snow to buy a bottle. There's no prescription or right way to heal—every person's path to healing will look different. There's also no guarantee you'll ever be completely healed, and even if you do experience an epiphany like I did, healing is not (and never will be) linear. Something might trigger you in the future. That is okay. Triggers can be your teachers. The only way to try to heal yourself so you can live this amazing life you so desperately want and deserve is by *acknowledgement*, not by avoidance.

I invite you to acknowledge what might be the root of some of the questionable choices and patterns in your dating life. If you've experienced trauma, whether of the Big T or small t variety, the time is now to begin the process of healing and facing what happened to you. The good news is that the light at the end of the tunnel is there, and while the tunnel itself is V. dark, scary, and generally *not* enjoyable, you must travel through it. Trust me, being out in the sunshine of inner peace feels a hell of a lot better than staying in the cold darkness of despair. The abundance of resources around you is astounding. Therapists, support groups, apps, and forums are all available to you right this instant. You are completely deserving of the life and love of your dreams, but the only way to get there is through the tunnel. Everyone's tunnel is different, so find what works for you and make the decision to quit avoiding it today. You are strong. **You are braver than you think.** You can only go up from here.

It's time to unshackle yourself from the past. As a reformed serial fuckboy dater and Big T Trauma survivor (now thriver), I know you can do it, and I believe in you. You can rewrite your own definitions because pain-free love *is* out there for you. I'll be your cheerleader from Netflix's *Cheer*, doing backflips from the sidelines, and cheering you on the entire way.

# Chapter 10—
# Swiping Right for All the Wrong Reasons

*Two things you will never have to chase: true friends and true love.*
*—Mandy Hale*

I am V. blessed to have a dad who should have repeatedly won awards for Father of The Year. While my behavior in my romantic relationships might have screamed: "She has daddy issues!" that wasn't exactly the case—at least not in the absent father sense. I was lucky enough to be raised by a man who was present in his marriage, took pride in his career, and somehow managed to snag two tickets to a Spice Girls concert and waited in line overnight for *NSYNC tickets (twice). Anyone who is fortunate enough to know my dad knows he is one hell of a guy, and, more importantly, one hell of a dad. While I wasn't struggling with the classic daddy issues, I did have a particular daddy issue that affected the bulk of my relationships well into adulthood: I had an irrational fear my daddy of the decade wouldn't be able to walk me down the aisle and give me away to the man of my dreams.

In an unfair karmic twist, I found out my dad had a brain tumor the night before my spring semester finals during my junior year of high school. I'm sure you can imagine how well a sixteen-year-old mega daddy's girl handled *that* news. While it (thankfully) wasn't a life-or-death situation at the time, it jolted me away from the garden variety problems a high school student typically deals with into a whole new way of thinking—one riddled with anxiety. This certainly was a trauma in my youth: having to face the thought of my dad's mortality—not exactly the usual topic of conversation in third period Chemistry. When I first got the news, I was beyond upset. My mind began to wonder, "What if my dad isn't here for _____?" Graduation, my first real job, and the biggest one of all—my wedding day. Why should a sixteen-year-old be thinking about her wedding day? (She shouldn't.) It took many years before I realized that sixteen-year-old me had become twenty-something me worrying about the same damn thing. My dad's brain tumor, which seemed to haunt my family every few years when a recommendation for another invasive surgery would be made, deeply affected me—particularly with regard to how I selected men to date.

Looking back, a significant number of my dating choices were the result of my (subconscious) desire to get married before my dad died. Not exactly a pattern daddio would be proud of. I stayed in relationships that were unhealthy, fell for fuckboys, and made a variety of other poor dating decisions in a desperate attempt to find someone who would finally get down on one knee. While marriage was certainly an end goal, finding someone who was just as perfect for me as I was for them is what I *should* have been focused on.

Believing in true love and marriage, I spent my twenties consumed with the idea of finding them. Desperately, I would ask myself if *this guy* could be the one or if *that guy* could just change _____, would he be the one? It was all because I was scared that:

a) I would never find someone,

or

b) my dad wouldn't get to see my wedding if I did.

Here are a few things I *should* have been scared of: marrying the wrong person, swiping right and wasting time with someone who wasn't worth my time, and, most importantly, not spending enough time with my parents when they needed me the most.

Our society puts a fuck ton of pressure on people to figure things out by a certain age. As a teenager, you're supposed to know what career will fulfill you until it's time to retire. By the time you reach your twenties, you're supposed to know what kind of person will make you happy for the rest of your life. If you *aren't* married or on baby number two by your thirties and forties, people start asking questions. Don't forget that you're supposed to do all of this and balance your career success at the same time. There is an enormous amount of pressure to adhere to this schedule of lifetime events—but our life is *not* an itinerary.

Marriage shouldn't have a timeline. Love shouldn't have a timeline. But, as humans, we're constantly trying to fit into a, you guessed it, mother-fucking timeline. Emotions don't know if it's 2022 or 1982. Emotions simply exist. I know people who have been in relationships for years and know less about their significant others than people who have been dating for two weeks. That's a harrowing reality about love: it doesn't give a damn about your timeline.

From a young age, most of us are taught love (you know, of the "real" variety) is associated with a specific timeline: boy meets girl; they fall in love; they date for a few years; they get engaged in their mid-twenties; they take a year to plan a wedding; they get married; they buy a house; they have 2.5 babies; they raise children; they retire; they die. Sorry to end on a morbid note, but hopefully you get the picture.

I was inundated with examples of said timeline—whether it was the adults around me when I was growing up or the couples I saw on TV and in movies or read about in books. Of course, everyone's relationship wasn't exactly the same, but they formed a collective expectation. At some point in our lives—usually when the dreaded middle-age is looming—most of us come to the harsh realization that this timeline, this outdated expectation, isn't remotely realistic for the majority of people on a quest to find "the one."

The reality is this: **there is no definitive timeline for epic love.** Love doesn't follow the rules. Love looks different for everyone. I'm sure there are millions of people who fell in love on the timeline I just described. Are they happy? I sure hope so. I'm also sure there are millions of others who went about it in a different manner. Are they happy? I also hope so, because it shouldn't matter when you fall in love—what matters is finding the right person for you.

We're all on our own timeline here. Some people want to be in a relationship for decades and never get married or have kids. That is okay. What *isn't* okay is judging someone else (or worse—yourself) for falling in love too soon or too late, getting married too quickly or never getting married at all, having babies before marriage or deciding kids aren't in the picture. Everything is okay as long as the two people who are involved agree. Isn't it beyond time to stop the comparisons and the one-size-fits-all expectations?

I get it—we can't just stop comparing ourselves to those around us. It's practically impossible in this age when society is focused on social media platforms where the idea that more followers = more popularity, and thousands of filters can make us look better than we do in real life. We mindlessly scroll through Instagram, TikTok, and Twitter seeing everyone else's lives before us. Most of the time, people aren't posting about the bad stuff—the failures or the losses—they are posting about the good parts of life: the successes, wins, engagements, weddings, and babies.

It's natural. Those are some amazing things to be proud of. It's also important to be proud of your failures and mistakes because those things also make you, *you*. And you, my darling, are beautiful just the way you are (there's even a song about it). It's important that we remind ourselves that we're on our own beautiful timeline, and it was designed just for us. Next time you're feeling like you aren't measuring up, that it's "too late" for you to do X or become Y, or to try whatever it is you want to try, give yourself a gentle reminder that you are *exactly* where you need to be. **It is never too late, and you are right on time.**

When we bring a certain timeline into the love equation, we are automatically setting ourselves up for failure. Let's run through a couple of scenarios, shall we?

Scenario number one: you know you're getting older, and you think you're running out of time to have kids or to fall in epic love.

Answer: age is, quite literally, just a fucking number. First of all, we are #blessed to live in a time when we have boatloads of technology at our fingertips. A woman can freeze her eggs plus there are facials, organic face peels, lasers, and facelifts—all to ensure that we stay looking fresh and can keep our options open for longer than ever before. Second, aging is not something to fear. I believe some of the most beautiful people in the world are the oldest among us. Older generations have so much wisdom and understanding. They have truly *lived.*

When I was fifteen, I happily embarked on my first job at a retirement community close to my parents' house. A couple of days a week, I would serve the residents in the communal dining room. It was an experience I cherish to this day. I remember noticing a variety of cliques: the popular girls, the jocks (being good at chess and, if they were lucky, golf), the outcasts, and the philosophers. While the parallels to my own high school experience were quite surprising, I also learned a great deal from the residents. My, what stories they all had. They spoke of times that I had learned about in AP History or watched in movies, but they had lived it. Their wisdom showed me a different kind of beauty I had never appreciated before—especially as a teenager. Age isn't something to fear, it's something to admire.

While society doesn't exactly make it easy (or fun) to live the single life beyond your twenties, settling down with someone shouldn't be a decision that's made because of how many candles are on your birthday cake. Plenty of people have found epic love later in life. Cameron Diaz married her beau, Benji Madden, at forty-two and later went on to become one hot mama at age forty-seven. Gwen Stefani and Blake Shelton have shown the world the beautiful possibilities of bouncing back and finding epic love post-divorce. Barbara Streisand and Josh Brolin married in their late fifties and have been happily married for over twenty years. There are so many more examples of this. Instead of worrying when you'll cross paths with this epic kind of love, focus on what a wonderful catch *you* are—one who is certainly worth the wait.

Look, our time on earth is finite, but we don't have to let that fact dictate how we live our lives or how or when we love. How awful would it be to be with someone, or worse, have children with someone, just because we thought time was running out? Or because we thought there were no other options? Let me tell you something: **there is always another option.** The Universe has a way of working things out in exactly the right way. You just need to believe it. Stop worrying about the how or the why—focus on the *what.* (You can pretend I'm Noah from *The Notebook.*) *What* do you want?! Do you want to meet your soulmate? Awesome! Stop worrying about how or when, and simply know that you *will.* Focus on what makes you happy and makes you the best you can be. I assure you, whether you are twenty-two or ninety-two, your soulmate is going to think you're the most beautiful person in the room.

"Too old" to have kids? There are ways around that if you're open to them. Maybe your person has kids of his or her own, and you are destined to be the perfect bonus parent. Or maybe you meet your person volunteering overseas and fall in love with the same child who needs a home, and you adopt that cute little girl three years later. There's an answer for everything—we're all just too busy trying to figure out what that answer is before it's ready for us, or more likely, before *we* are ready for *it.* When we take the worry and stress about time out of the equation, we can finally start to enjoy life as it is.

There's also no need to stay upset about "wasting time" in a relationship that wasn't right; perhaps you needed to go through that relationship to grow and to learn something. That something might be that you don't want to feel like that ever again. No one goes into a relationship or marriage expecting it to fail. We all plan on forever, but sometimes, for one reason or another, forever doesn't happen. While it might be enjoyable to think of what could have been if you hadn't "wasted your time" with your ex who cheated on you as a newlywed, it won't do much to benefit you and all that is to come. You can divorce your ex, but you can't annul the past like it never happened in the first place; however, you always have the power to create any future you want.

Scenario number two: you stay with someone who treats you badly or simply isn't right for you because you can't believe there is someone else out there who could possibly love you after this.

Answer: Honey, if there is one thing you need to know right now, it's this: **there will always be someone who will love you.** Age doesn't matter. Wrinkles don't matter. Clothing brands don't matter. Love is love, baby, and, again, age ain't nothing but a number. Have you ever stayed with someone, even though you knew in your heart of hearts that that person was *not* the shit, and most importantly, not the right person for you? Life can be a scary, confusing, total mindfuck of a thing, and most of the time, we have no idea what we're doing. It's a series of trials and errors in hopes of finding something that works—dating and relationships included.

Scared to be alone forever? Let's pretend you never meet your soulmate, or the person you wouldn't mind being in epic love with for the rest of your life. Would you:

a) prefer to stay in a sixty-year marriage with some annoying fool who disagrees with you 75% of the time and annoys you to your core

or

b) prefer to leave that annoying fool in the dust, pick up three fun hobbies, spend time with your family, make friends that turn into family, and live a pretty cool life, despite not having someone to share it with?

I'm going to go out on a limb here and say that most of the non-masochists reading this book went with option b, because who wants to be *that* unhappy for *that* long? Hopefully no one. It's easy to feel stuck and become complacent, especially when life can feel so hard to deal with on your own. Remember: **you aren't alone unless you make yourself be alone.** Close friendships can fill your soul in the most amazing way. It is so important to nurture your friendships, especially when a new romance is blossoming. Your good friendships are a part of you. Never, under any circumstances, should you let them go. When you have those kinds of friendships, you will never be alone.

Of course, there will be moments when you will be *physically* alone; but you don't need to torture yourself and turn it into a colossal mental breakdown and assume you will be alone forever. Instead, try a different approach: enjoy the simplicity and peacefulness of cooking dinner for yourself. Enjoy the ability to treat yourself to a facial and a massage (or whatever makes you happy) whenever you damn well please. Enjoy the silence—understand it, and, most importantly, learn to love it! There's no need to be anxious about being the only single person at the Christmas party because it's a party, you're surrounded by great music and great people (hopefully), and there is probably an open bar. Furthermore, **there is absolutely nothing wrong with being single.** There is, however, something wrong with staying in a bad relationship just for the sake of not being single.

*Fried Green Tomatoes,* besides being an absolutely delicious salad, has been a favorite movie of mine since I was a young girl. During the film, there's a poignant line that hits me in my core: "I wonder how many people don't get the one they want but end up with the person they're supposed to be with." All too often, we're focused on our wants and how to get there. For me, I wanted a husband because I wanted my dad to watch me get married. This desire, coupled with my unhealed traumas, dictated just about every dating decision I made for a decade. Here I am, a decade later, a tiny bit wiser, and guess what. I ended up with the person I am *supposed* to be with.

Can you imagine what might have happened if I had given Mr. Bartender a second chance, expected a real-lationship with The Comedian, or been fully honest with Smooth? My seemingly "bad" past dating decisions were part of my divine timeline, which ultimately led me to exactly where I needed to be exactly *when* I needed to be there. Once I became certain about what I wanted and left the *how* and the *who* out of the equation, the Universe brought the perfect man into my life. Time is linear but life is not. Stop restricting yourself because of time, and live! Do what you want when you want. Strive to be a better version of yourself every day, not only because you never know what day is going to be your last, but also because you should always want to be the best you can be and live the best damn life you can.

Is life too short? Sure. It would be great to be a hot twenty-something forever; but I would imagine it would get old (pun intended) after a while. Life, as short as it is, can be as wonderful as you make it. Figure out what you want and what sets your soul on fire and chase it. Chase it every damn day, in every way possible, and you'll begin to see how time never really mattered in the first place.

# Chapter 11—
# You Can't Change Your Past, but You Can Create Your Future

*When we think we have been hurt by someone in the past, we build up defenses to protect ourselves from being hurt in the future. So the fearful past causes a fearful future and the past and future become one.*
*—Gerald G. Jampolsky*

While I was unknowingly hanging on to the men who assaulted and abused me, I was also clinging to a boy I dated in high school. If you think I was crazy for letting a teenaged boy affect my romantic relationships in my twenties, I could not agree more. I should clarify that by "boyfriend" I really mean we worked together, flirted a bunch over text, and occasionally made out in his car. We never defined the relationship. Going back to chapter 1's revelation: do not, under any circumstances, get your tender heartstrings involved when there isn't agreement from both parties that it is an exclusive relationship. It never ends well, regardless of how many years you've been around the sun. While high school isn't the ideal place to start a serious relationship, the rule still applies. **If your heart gets involved with someone who didn't want it in the first place, it's *not* going to end in your favor.**

Despite going to the same high school and playing the same sport, I didn't get to know this fellow until we met at Jamba Juice.

It wasn't a serendipitous "OMG, I'm so sorry I took the wrong smoothie!" kind of meeting. We met because we were scheduled for the same shift at our part time jobs. Glamorous, right? Despite having a ton of fun in the frozen fruit section, homeboy never acknowledged me at school, even in the middle of volleyball practice. Even when we were on the same team, he wouldn't look in my direction, which was a warning sign that I all too happily ignored. Alas, my sixteen-year-old self (in true teenager fashion) caught feelings for a boy who wanted nothing more than attention from the varsity cheerleading team and to pass Honors English with a C minus.

Flash forward to our Jamba Juice Christmas party. I was desperately trying to locate the bathroom and opened a door to find my "boyfriend" playing tonsil hockey with one of my (formerly) favorite co-workers. This was definitely a case of V. small t trauma, but it affected me for years to come. Infidelity in a relationship is traumatic, whether it's a thirty-year marriage, or a case of high school puppy love. Of course, the repercussions will be more jarring if a marriage or long-term relationship is affected, but this is a reality about trauma: everyone reacts differently and may hold on to things; it doesn't matter if the reaction doesn't make any sense to someone else. This act, perpetrated by a horny, awful-at-communicating teenaged boy, caused me to behave as though all my subsequent relationships would end with the same fate. Subconsciously, I believed this and therefore attracted men who were prone to the same behavior.

It's likely you'll fall victim to someone who is emotionally unavailable, and it will make you doubt your belief in the possibility of a healthy relationship. Bad relationships can change your definition of what love is. After a bad experience, you may be on guard with overly heightened senses, walls all the way up, and a padlock at the entrance, ultimately expecting the bad stuff that's happened over and over again to happen *one more time.*

The truth is this: we simply need to do a better job dating. By "better" I mean we need to be *more selective* of the people we choose to spend our time with. We need to do better for ourselves because we deserve better. We also need to continue to hold firm to our non-negotiables—our list of necessary qualities in a mate—even (*especially*) when we feel lonely. If we're feeling lonely, we are much more likely to bend our own rules just for the sake of getting affection. I know I dated some guys who were really not worth my time just to get some compliments, some cuddles, and, well, some good old-fashioned cock. After being single for a long time, I missed the three C's! If you've been single for a hot minute and gone on Lord-knows-how-many dates, I'm guessing you understand this dilemma. While your intuition is telling you it's going to end in flames, you're like, "HIT IT!"—pressing the jukebox and ready to get it on.

More important than our penchant for lowering our standards when we're lonely is how we act when we meet the unicorn of the modern dating world: a keeper. Of course, we're like, "Are you for real? I mean, what's wrong with you? Surely, you're too good to be true!" From there, we typically sabotage what could be the exact relationship we've been looking for by expecting something to go wrong because that's what happened last time. When you expect something to go wrong, it's somehow going to go wrong, even if the Universe was sending you a little miraculous reminder that good people, in fact, still exist. We're sometimes so busy living in the past that we let our jadedness get in the way of everything we so badly desire.

Imagine you meet one of these unicorns: a genuine keeper. Things are going great, and then one day when the unicorn is enjoying a night out on the town with its homies, kissing puppies and chasing rainbows, or whatever it is unicorns do when they're together, you freak out because your unicorn hasn't texted you back. Your mind takes you down the rabbit hole of your past because your ex, who didn't respond to your text when they were "with their friends", was actually getting down and dirty at a really nice hotel with their new co-worker they told you not to worry about. You're triggered. You're worried. You're freaking the fuck out because—of course—this would happen to you again. Meanwhile, the poor unicorn is just hanging out at a twenty-four-hour breakfast joint with a dead phone, laughing it up with its friends, and eating a late-night omelet because it sounded good at the time.

When your unicorn finally charges its phone and sees the twenty-eight missed calls and fifteen text messages from your freaking-out self, it might also see a few giant red flags. How do you deal with this situation? You could explain that you've been hurt before, mention that unanswered texts are a trigger for you, and ask for a check-in text every couple of hours. This kind of communication is key in every single relationship, but trust is equally important.

Unfortunately, we cannot change what happened to us in the past. It's set in stone—a chapter in the history book of our dating life. What we *can* do is acknowledge our experience(s) and promise ourselves that just because our ex was a jerk that doesn't mean that everyone we date in the future will be. **Every new relationship**

**should be treated as a clean slate.** This doesn't mean that our baggage doesn't come with us because, well, we're stuck with it forever. It does mean that our baggage can be neatly stored in a closet while we focus on keeping the rest of our house clean. Where your focus grows, energy flows. In other words, stop letting your past get in the way of your future and accept that while a jerk cheated on you one, two, or seventeen years ago, it doesn't mean that the person you meet now will too.

Instead of focusing on what could go wrong, it's imperative to focus on what could go *right*. Does this mean that from now on, every single thing in your life will be so amazing you want to get up and sing? Sadly, no; but a lot more positive things will come into your life, and when the bad stuff does come up, it won't define your whole reality. Entering a new relationship can be unnerving—especially if you've been burned in the past. You're getting to know this person and trying to figure out if they're someone you'd like to keep in your life full-time. The speed at which this happens is different for everyone. Some people are fine jumping right in, while others prefer dipping their toes in the water first. Neither approach is better than the other as long as both parties are:

a) willing to keep the past in the past

and

b) open to the abundance of the future.

Take it from the girl who let her teenaged self dictate the course of the faux-lationships of her twenties: it's not worth it. I'm sure we all have scars from our past. What if we wore our scars as badges of honor instead of shields of shame? What if we treated them like evidence that we're veterans of something way bigger? Imagine the power we would have if we weren't so ashamed of these parts of ourselves. There would be no reason to be afraid to talk about our past because we would know that's what made us who we are today (and who you are today is worthy of, ahem, *ev-er-y-thing*). They say beauty is pain, but if you ask me, I think pain can be beautiful if we can realize how strong we have become as a result of it—and even if we don't *feel* strong, the fact that we are still standing is the proof. **Our pain can lead us to our purpose.**

You don't have to be in pain forever, okay? That said, you do have to lean into it a bit to feel some things you might not have accepted when whatever hurt you took place. Take down your shield of shame, pop open a bottle of rosé, watch one of your favorite movies that makes you feel all the feels, and let it all come out. You've got to let it out before an amazing partner can truly get in. Who knows, said partner might watch reruns of *The Vampire Diaries* with you on Sunday (without complaining), always think you're the hottest thing in the room, and make you laugh until you cry. Don't scare *that* person away because you think they're just like the rest.

Is there a fuck ton of jerks in the current dating pool? Yes, I won't deny that and even if I tried, the evidence is out there in plain sight on Tinder, Bumble, and Hinge. There is also a fuck ton of amazing, emotionally available people. **There is a fuck ton of single people in our world.** Catching Daniel from Hinge cheating on you after you've been together for a year or seeing Tayler from Tinder back on Tinder when you agreed to be exclusive are not fun things. Both of those jackasses suck beyond words. You, however, *don't* suck and thank the high heavens it didn't go any further with either of them. Just because they turned out to be losers not worth an ounce of your precious time doesn't mean that every person you meet will be.

Not allowing the past to affect your present (or future) is often no easy feat. Trusting someone new—or even trusting yourself—after betrayal can feel impossible and scary. While you can breakup with someone who betrayed you, you can't do the same when it feels like you've betrayed yourself. First, take as much time as you need to rebuild the trust you have with *yourself.* By nurturing the relationship you have with yourself, you can begin to restore faith in your ability to make decisions that align with your ideals—such as recognizing people who are worthy of your trust. When that trust is restored, it might feel less overwhelming to begin trusting other people once more. The power you need lies within you—pretty cool, right?

# Chapter 12—
# The Art of Keeping It in Your Pants

*What's a fuck when what I want is love?*
*—Henry Miller*

Sex. Getting it on. Doing the deed. The Waikiki sneaky between the cheeky. Whatever you want to call it, sex is a V. important factor when it comes to dating. Whether you like it or not, sex sells, baby! If you disagree, I'd like to invite you to consider the fact that most dating apps are initially based on one thing: sexual attraction. You typically don't swipe right for someone you're *not* attracted to. There was never a time when I was on Bumble looking through all the men in my vicinity that I thought, "Oh, yes, definitely going to give this guy a shot" when there was nothing about his appearance, or even the little I could deduce about his personality, that sparked my interest. Things can get even more complicated as I'm sure you know. Just because you're attracted to someone in photos doesn't mean sparks will fly in person. Alternatively, just because you're not attracted to someone in photos doesn't mean sparks *won't* fly in person. I know looks fade and a lackluster personality is (usually) forever. Personality and connection are key, but so is physical attraction. You want to have hot sex with the person you're with, right? You're probably not having hot sex with someone you aren't attracted to.

Sex is important. Deciding *when* to have it is also important. It can be *really* hard to keep it in your pants when you're super attracted to someone, having an amazing date, they're saying all the right things, and this connection just feels different. It also doesn't help when said date consists of maybe one or four too many glasses of vino. Don't worry, we've all been there and done that, including yours truly. I definitely could have been better about practicing the good old-fashioned art of keeping it in one's pants in chapters 1 through 6.

If I had just played it cool and listened to my brain instead of my vagina, I would have saved a lot, and I mean a *yacht load*, of tears. And wine. And truffle fries, which I consumed on Sunday nights like they were a food group. Can you imagine if I decided to *not* go for it with Mr. East Coast those two weekends? We likely never would have met in person in the first place. We'd probably have stopped talking on the phone, and whatever faux-lationship we might have had would have fizzled into oblivion because we didn't have much in common and certainly were not compatible. I would have been absolutely fine, albeit a bit bummed at first, and moved on without having my momentous meltdown.

What about Sir L. B.? Remember him? (BTW, he comes back again soon.) What if I refused to give it up until he made it official between us? What if, when he didn't make it official (because he was not looking for official-ness), I had been like, "Bro, I'm out" and gone on my semi-merry little way. I say semi-merry because he was a really good dude, and we did have a good time together. Sex? It just made me fall for him much faster and harder and gave him a good reason to keep me around. What can I say? I was happy to give a fantastic blow job (but only to a guy who wasn't sticking his wiener in other women's mouths).

I realized that if I was having sex with a guy without any exclusivity tied to it, he was going to keep me around, whether he saw a future with me or not. Why? Because I was having sex with him, it felt really good, and he had *zero* responsibility to be my boyfriend. As the saying goes: "Why buy the cow when you can get the milk for free?" Although I don't have a copy myself, I'm pretty sure the fuckboy handbook states something along the lines of: "Why settle down when I can get the pussy for free?" It was a hard pill to swallow.

Here's what I learned about sex and dating: the moment I had sex with a man before the relationship was defined, he unchecked his mental box labeled "potential wife material" and filed me under the "well-she's-a-lot-of-fun-and-gives-a-great-blowjob-maybe-I'll-keep-her-around-but-nothing-serious" file. Not exactly ideal, right? Even if we had been on the most spectacular, life-changing, magical first, second, or whatever date in the history of the Universe, I might no longer be considered front-runner wife material, and he would likely continue to explore other options. He'd keep me around because I was getting his dick wet with no commitment required, but eventually he'd either ghost me or dump me. It's literally every fuckboy's dream. Even if I had been the absolute best version of myself, I was no longer classified in his mind as anything serious.

Picture it: I'm on date lucky-number-three with Michael B. Jordan's doppelganger (including abs a la *Creed II*) who just so happens to be an excruciatingly handsome prince, ridiculously smart, and able to hold an intriguing conversation. He knows what wine to order with dinner, he's dressed immaculately, and he is V. interested. He's telling me all the right things, like how I'm *everything* he has been looking for in a girl, and I'm so beautiful, and funny, and . . . what do I do?

Knowing what I know now, I'd tell myself to *not* go home with the guy, to *not* order more drinks, and to *not* do *an-y-thing* that could potentially risk clouding my otherwise spot-on judgment and get me into a situation where the inevitable fireworks of a kiss at the end of the night turn into a full-blown heavy make out session on his couch, and the next thing I know it's three o'clock in the morning, and I'm staring at my mascara-stained eyes in the mirror thinking I've met the perfect man and that this is it.

Sex is awesome. (V. awesome). It's even more awesome when it's with someone you're wildly attracted to who is all-of-the-things. What isn't awesome, in my opinion, is having sex with someone who doesn't know my middle name, doesn't know how I like my coffee in the morning (or if I hate coffee), or, *most importantly,* is having sex with other people. If I had known that Prince Doppelganger of Jordan was sleeping with other women and telling them exactly the same things he was telling me, I probably wouldn't have had sex with the guy. A serious question to ask yourself is: do you want to be one of possibly sev-er-al other people that's sharing the same body? When I began honestly asking myself that question, things changed. This is when exclusivity comes into play.

Exclusivity may not be what you're looking for at this point in your life, and that's absolutely okay. It's *your* body, and you hold the power to choose what you do and don't want to do with it. The same goes with your heart. If you're like me and find that sex only makes your heart get more involved, it might not be a bad idea to try this whole "keep it in your pants" practice, and hold off on any naked passions until you're sure you're *both* interested in the same thing.

How do we know when the time is right? Unfortunately, there is no magic formula. It could happen on date number one (rare and I probably wouldn't risk it), three, or seventy-eight (yikes!). It's worth waiting until you're both on the same page about wanting to be in a committed relationship. That's when you can let your freak flag fly and show what a fox you are in bed.

Hard? Yep.

Important? Ab-so-fuck-ing-lute-ly.

In a culture that's obsessed with sex, it's V. hard to wait, especially when your old M.O. was to throw caution to the wind and just go for it when it felt right. Feeling right is definitely important, but for me it was way more valuable—and ensured my poor little heart strings didn't get taken advantage of—to lock my pussy up until I got a commitment. I realize this isn't a novel concept, but it took me a while to realize that a surefire way to keep my heart from getting hurt by a fuckboy is to not sleep with him until he commits. **A fuckboy isn't going to commit.** He's going to find another girl who will willingly have (casual) sex with him.

I learned that an emotionally available, secure gentleman wouldn't walk away from me if I pumped the brakes when things got a little heated. If someone is into you, they'll keep coming back. When they come back, you can show them all of the amazing things about you *besides* your ability to make them orgasm in a minute, and they'll probably think something along the lines of, "Damn, I really like this person." And then they won't want anyone else to date you. And then the two of you can define the relationship in one way or another and have sex like rabbits for the next six months. The timeline will vary, of course, but a person with serious potential will not be deterred if you want to take things slow. If anything, it'll make them want you—seriously—*even more.* Use it to your advantage and show off everything (else) about you that makes you, you.

If you're staring at this page, semi-scoffing, and wondering how casual sex plays into this, let me make it crystal clear: I'm not hating on casual sex. If that's what you want, and it makes you happy, I say go for it! (Hopefully with a condom because STDs are a V. real thing.) Seriously, whatever works for you, boo! Keep in mind, it is *very* easy to catch feelings when you have amazing sex with someone. If that happens, it's going to sting if you find out they're not interested in anything beyond sex. In other words, be careful with your emotions, okay? K.

If I had followed my own advice, I would have saved myself so much heartbreak and *so* much wine. Sex adds another level to a connection with your partner. I, like many women, tend to be more emotionally invested once I've had sex with someone, particularly with someone I like and/or have a serious attraction to.

I think I had sex earlier than I should have, or even wanted to, because I was scared I would lose such a "catch" if I didn't give him *the V.* I thought that if my personality wasn't enough to keep him around, a roll in the hay would definitely keep him interested. Unfortunately, this couldn't be further from the truth. Once I decided that I wouldn't mind losing a guy if he moved on when I didn't give him the keys to my undercarriage, I reclaimed my power. If he wants to leave, good! Now I know what he was most interested in. I don't want to be loved for my vagina or prowess in bed. I want to be loved for my intelligence, my spunk, my passion, and my drive. Of course, I also want him to love my body and think I'm a 10 in the sack but only *after* he's discovered the other stuff.

One of the most important acknowledgements I had to face was that I didn't have to lead with sex as if it was my best quality. Love isn't sex, even though, because of what happened to me, I believed that to be true. Even if you're a porn star and being really good in bed is one of your biggest claims to fame, I am sure you want to be loved and committed to for something other than the tricks you have up your sleeve in the bedroom. One of the biggest not-so-secret secrets I uncovered in freeing myself from fuckboys was to **practice the art of keeping it in your pants**. Fuckboys, even the ones cleverly disguised as well-dressed M. B. J. doppelgangers, fled the moment they realized I was only interested in something serious and wasn't willing to give it up on the first, second, or third (etc.) date.

I acknowledge that I hold a lot of power down below, but I am worth so much more than that. What is more important to you? Finding a meaningful, passionate, committed, and hot-sex-all-the-time relationship or giving in to your primal desires a wee bit too soon and potentially losing any chance for something more serious than sex and late night "u up?" texts? My mantra? My gorgeous vagina deserves nothing less than five-star sex with a man who tells me how much he loves me (and my vagina).

What will your mantra be?

# Chapter 13—
# Falling in Epic Love with . . .
# Yourself

*Give yourself the love you seek, and the universe will send people who match it.*
*—Abraham Hicks*

For many, college is a time to experiment with a bunch of new things, find out more about yourself, and hopefully make it to your classes on time. While I expected to have a variety of new experiences when I left my childhood home for my parents' alma mater (which was also my dream school), I certainly did not expect this: three weeks after moving in, one of my newest and closest college friends—who also happened to be of the opposite sex—walked into my dorm room, tossed me a vibrator, and bluntly yelled, "This'll help you feel better!" as he headed off to his afternoon Psychology lecture. I know what you're wondering and, don't worry, the packaging was fully intact. My confidence, however, was not.

Make me feel . . . *better?* What was even wrong with me? I hadn't yet had my traumatizing encounter with The Freshman Fuckboy. I wasn't nursing some premature heartbreak or reeling after a first date gone awfully awry. Hell, it was my first semester at college, and I barely knew the location of my classes, let alone the location of any eligible bachelors who might be interested in a shy freshman (who had to google what a vibrator was). What did I do to make a new acquaintance think the best medicine for me was a good old-fashioned, self-induced orgasm instead of a keg stand like every other college student? Clearly something was terribly wrong, because Brandon from the second level of my dorm tower just walked in with a sparkly purple rabbit that supposedly could make one levitate into oblivion. I'll spare you the details of my test ride of this miracle worker slash instant mood changer. Let's just say, there's a reason for the five-star Amazon reviews. And I absolutely levitated.

To this day, I still have zero clue as to why I was gifted a vibrating dildo with rabbit ears from a guy I had essentially just met, but the point of the story is that homeboy was kind of . . . spot on (the pun is definitely intended). It did make me feel better. Way better. Frankly, I could have listed off every capital of every country in the world after that release, and I have never been much of a geography buff. Orgasms: they make you feel better, whether they happen by yourself, with someone else, or with a battery-operated, sparkly purple vibrating dildo with faux rabbit ears.

After my bizarre introduction to self-care, I fully embraced the concept moving forward. Before you start thinking that I was a masturbating machine (although there was a lot of masturbation in my twenties, and it's about damn time we started normalizing it), my idea of self-care extended to other areas of the physical realm. I actively sought it out and began to regularly incorporate it into my life. PSA: while self-care can include things to enhance how your body looks to yourself or others, it also goes far beyond improving your physical appearance. It is *anything* that you do that boosts your physical, mental, or emotional well-being.

Botox? Um . . . Hell. To. The. Yeah. To me, Botox is one of the greatest inventions. Like, ever. Shout out to those of you who don't need or want it, but I'm at the point where I run to the chair and shout to the injector, "Frozen, LIKE . . . ELSA FROZEN!!!"

Massages? Oh-my-goodness-yes-please! And preferably by a massage therapist who is Zac Efron's long lost twin and who offers me champagne prior to rolling out the ten thousand knots in my neck and shoulders with his perfectly chiseled arms.

Workout Classes? God damn it, Diane, my ass looks amazing because of you! I really hate spending seventy-five dollars on this, but there's no denying my peach looks extra perky these days!

"Quick" runs to Target to "pick up a few things?" Is there anything better?! (There isn't; unless Target starts setting up wine and charcuterie bars in their stores.)

Sometimes you need to give yourself permission to take a bath, go for a lunchtime walk, or actually use a PTO or sick day (or just a mental health day). Grant yourself radical permission to do something that makes you feel genuinely good.

In addition to doing some things for yourself, sometimes it's just as important to *not* do some things for yourself. Have you ever said "no" to something or someone that would have otherwise caused you stress if you hadn't? This can be one of the most liberating feelings in the world! Trust me, as a (semi) reformed people pleaser, there's no point in making someone else happy if it comes at the expense of your wellbeing. Boundaries: they're important AF.

Clearly, there are tons of things we can do to care for ourselves. And that's important and necessary at times. There's no denying the fact that it *feels* good to look good, and we should all treat our physical selves once in a while. You know what's also essential and *way* more important? Focusing on our thoughts. **All of this starts and ends with you.** The ball is in your metaphorical court, which just so happens to be your mind.

Go ahead and think about your day today, whether it's 6 a.m. or 11 p.m. How have you been talking to yourself today? By talking to yourself, I don't mean shouting at yourself on a street corner like someone on drugs. I mean your internal thoughts. We all have them, and we have them *all* the time. Have you been kind, gracious, forgiving, loving, and motivating toward yourself or have you been a big, stinking, thinking pile of not-again-you-disgusting-heathen-how-could-you-have-done-this-again?!

The number of self-deprecating thoughts I used to have on a consistent basis was pretty fucking terrifying. I looked in the mirror and broke my body apart like I was Tyra Banks analyzing someone on *America's Next Top Model.* Note: I am not a model. If I made a mistake, I crucified myself for not getting it right. Note: everyone, and I mean ev-er-y-one, makes mistakes (it's called being human). Eventually, I talked myself out of new challenges because I became convinced I would fail. Note: the best way to prove you can't do something is by never trying.

I realized that all the work I was doing on my physical self was completely pointless because the person on the inside was a self-sabotaging, critical, loathing jerk. Who wants to be around *that* kind of energy? It was like I was driving around in a brand, spanking new Porsche Cayenne that was filled to the brim with trash and rotten food. No one, not a damn soul, is interested in taking the passenger seat in that ride, you feel me? How could I have spent thousands of dollars on skincare, workout classes, and other nice things yet couldn't spend a second loving . . . myself? Self-care and self-love are two totally different things. There is zero point in taking great care of your physical self if you don't love the person you're taking care of which is, you know, *you*. It's also pretty pointless to love yourself if you don't even know who you really are.

I had spent decades treating myself to this and that, occasionally liking myself (usually when I succeeded at something or received praise from someone around me), and generally not knowing who the hell I was. I was a version of Mikaela I thought I needed to be in order to be loved and admired. I acted how I thought I needed to act to get people to like me. No wonder I didn't fully love myself. I wasn't even being myself! My higher self was probably scoffing, "Hellooooooo. I'm right here. Don't you know you can be so much more you?" while I was traipsing around, being this mediocre version of myself, wondering why I didn't have the confidence of Blake Lively. Living off external validation was never going to make me fully happy.

I recognized I would never be Blake Lively. I know. What a (not so) shocking revelation. But seriously, all too often we're desperately trying to be an orange when we're really a pineapple. Although both are delicious tropical fruits, one is orange and round while the other one is yellow with a green, pointy top. Step one to self-love: stop trying to be like everyone else and start being you (you know, the real you, the inner you, the badass you who has been screaming to be let out of the cage like a lion around dinnertime). I know now that my self-worth needs to come from me. Nobody's opinion or validation—other than my own—matters. Not even Chris Hemsworth's or Oprah's. Just mine: Mikaela Kostaras's.

Scared because you don't think people will like you? Yes, it is V. scary. Worst case scenario: some people don't like you, but one person who you never knew before is all, "OMG I totally dig your vibe" and you're like, "OMG really?" (And they really do.) I promise, it's way fucking better to be loved for the *real* you (even if it's only by one person and that person is you) than to be loved by many when you're putting on an act. I'm sure with the current world population, the odds of more than one person liking the real you are certainly high. Cardi B isn't everyone's cup of tea, but that badass bitch is laughing all the way to the bank with a sweet following of a shit ton of people who think she's all that and a bag of chips.

Your top concern shouldn't be whether other people like you or not. It should be whether *you* like yourself or not. Your sole purpose in your lifetime on earth is not to be loved by other people—your objective is much, much greater than winning that kind of popularity contest. You're here to love yourself and blaze your own, unique trail—a trail no one else could possibly light up so beautifully.

So, how do you love yourself? Figure out who the fuck you are and what the fuck makes you seriously happy. Do more of those things and celebrate yourself as you do it. Congratulate yourself for being awesome. Pat yourself on the back for all your wins—big and small. Give yourself a warm hug when you lose. You can't break up with yourself, so you might as well learn to love the fuck out of the person gazing back at you in the mirror.

Once I had a better idea of who-the-hell-I-actually-was versus who-I-was-desperately-trying-to-be, I made an effort to be nice to this oddly familiar stranger in my life. Speaking from experience, when you've only half liked yourself for decades, you're not going to instantly become a happy-go-lucky, I-shit-sparkles-for-breakfast fairy in twenty-four hours. It takes time, and inevitably negative thoughts will pop into your brain no matter what you do. You're going to mess up, fall, succeed, trip over greatness, fail, and everything in between. And that's okay.

All day, every day, remind yourself of a singular truth: you're the greatest person you've ever met, and you love the hell out of you because you're you. There's not one other person in the world who can say that because, you know, they aren't you. How fucking awesome is that?

Step two to self-love: love yourself regardless of the outcome. It's easy to say nice things to yourself when you're killing the game and batting a thousand (or you know, whatever a good percentage in baseball is. I honestly have zero idea). It's *not* so easy to say nice things to yourself when you totally messed up and lost a zillion dollars, and your hair looks like a bunch of bats found their newest place to hang out. But that's the *most* important time to treat yourself with some extra mental hugs and kisses. You've got to remind yourself all the damn time of how great you are and how deserving you are because, well, you *are*. And make it a must-do to do something you love, whether it's writing, singing, dancing, drawing, walking your dog, vacuuming . . . whatever.

Make a habit of listening to your thoughts. Bad ones will inevitably come up, especially when life is throwing you curveballs like it is 2020 all over again. Acknowledge those bad thoughts and question what triggered them, but don't buy into the story. Allow yourself to feel whatever it is you're feeling without letting it consume you for days on end. Once you've worked through the negative feelings and questioned their truth, remind yourself of how great you are because you are being you and no one else can say that! If this doesn't come naturally for you, try talking to yourself as you would talk to your best friend or your dog. You wouldn't chastise them for every misstep, right? Treat yourself with just as much compassion, grace, and acceptance as you would those you truly care about. If you want epic love outside of yourself, it must start inside of yourself.

Honestly, so many people are trying to be what they think other people want. Imagine if that wasn't the case, and everyone was genuine, authentic, and totally loving toward themselves. For starters, there would be way fewer trolls on Instagram and Twitter.

The best part of loving yourself unapologetically and habitually is reminding yourself that there is no one, lit-er-al-ly nobody on this planet, who is you. I don't know what the current world population is, but I'm pretty sure it's equivalent to a million fuck tons of people. And out of a million fuck tons of people there is *one* you. *Uno. Un. Ein. Yksi.* That makes you really fucking special, okay? Relish that for a minute. Ruminate on the fact that you have the unique opportunity to be you right here, right now. Do you want to continue being like every other person, or do you want to be you? This is a PSA to love yourself—the *real* you—with and without a vibrator and regardless of what other people think.

# Chapter 14—
# Your Biggest Frenemy Is Your Ego

*When you connect to the silence within you, that is when you can make sense of the disturbance going on around you.*
*—Stephen Richards*

I'm going to go ahead and address the elephant in our metaphorical room: I, Mikaela Kostaras, have been V. guilty of staying in relationships that weren't worth a millisecond of my life. While you're now familiar with Mr. East Coast and The Bartender, I assure you I could have written several more chapters to prove this point.

The reason I didn't bore you to death with chapter after chapter of me repeating the same mistake over and over again (with a different guy and usually in a different state) is because the point of this book isn't about the mistakes, it's the *reasons* I made them and the breakthroughs I had as a result. Why was I continuously dating emotionally unavailable men who were way more interested in what was between my legs than what was between my ears? Beyond the traumas, it was because I became used to that kind of faux-lationship. Deep down, I knew how it would inevitably play out because I was only allowing one kind of guy into my life and, ultimately, heart. I felt safe dating these men because there was no uncertainty about how or when it would end. Feeling in control post trauma is *everything.* I was also validating the falsehood I had come to believe as true: that love meant sex and pain—a definition that certainly needed to be changed.

It seems masochistic, right? Why would I knowingly date crappy fuckboys instead of getting out of my fucked-up comfort zone and shooting my shot with the educated, handsome, 11/10 guy I kept seeing at the Starbucks? Because my ego wasn't comfortable with me playing that big. My ego was afraid to let me step out of my comfort zone—a zone that gave fuckboys the FastPass to my already battered heart.

What in the actual fuck is the ego and what in the actual fuck did it have to do with my formerly crappy taste in men? Well, it had *everything* to do with it. Your ego is the part of you that plays small, plays it safe, and holds you back from the cutie at the coffee shop because it doesn't like things that are uncertain, unfamiliar, and outside the realm of what it thinks is possible. Its main goal is to protect you, and it wants to kinda-sorta-totally keep you exactly right where you are because:

a) it's V. comfortable,
b) it's not scary,
and
c) it's V. predictable.

The ego doesn't sound all that great, right? Well, it's a part of us and is here to stay, so we have to learn how to tame it and tap into the higher self. Your higher self fully believes you are worthy of everything you desire and is absolutely certain you are capable of getting just that. Personally, my higher self totally knew I not only could attract said cutie from the coffee shop, but that I was also totally worthy of an amazing man who was emotionally available and able to hold a conversation about things beyond when we'd be hitting the sheets. I don't know about you, but I really wanted to stop dating total losers, like, many, many years ago.

How do you know if you're letting the good ole ego in the driver's seat of your dating life? Well, if you're like me, you're staying in unfulfilling relationships with losers who aren't worth a double take, let alone months or years of your life. Or you could just be dating the same kind of person repeatedly. They could be controlling, emotionally unavailable, or abusive. Although it seems V. counterintuitive, your ego will want you to keep falling in love with the same person—albeit with a different face—over and over again because it knows exactly what will happen. It has the playbook for what's going to go down, like it's a numbered list on a Microsoft Word document. Here's what my list looked like:

1. Meet cutie.
2. Have amazing first date.
3. Have sex.
4. Fall in ~~love~~ lust.
5. Keep having sex, believing he will change, see how great I am, and propose in a year because I'm the best thing that ever happened to him.
6. Get upset because nothing is happening and wonder what I'm doing wrong.

7. Give him an ultimatum.
8. Things end; I hate him.
9. I'm alone again, a year older, and more jaded than I was twelve months ago.
10. Repeat.

See what I mean? I was going through the same steps every time but expecting a different result. That is insane. I was getting in my own way. How could this have happened?!

Well, my traumas were a driving factor behind the whole unworthiness thing. But beyond healing from them, I realized I also needed to throw my ego in the backseat. It was time to let my higher self in the driver's seat and let it drive like I was trying to beat Lewis Hamilton in a Formula One race. (I, too, wonder how I became the woman who uses a sports reference in her book about fuckboys, and the answer to that question is *marriage*.) My higher self dreams big, thinks bigger, knows how abundant the world is, and believes I am totally deserving of freakishly amazing things. Your higher self is shouting "You're doing amazing, sweetie!" while you're out and about, living your fabulous life, being your fabulous self, and attracting all-the-fabulous people into your realm. Your higher self is totally connected to the Universe. Wouldn't it be awesome to be connected to the source of all-things-amazing and limitless abundance?

It sounds fantastic, but if you're anything like me, who spent decades listening to my ego and operating from a place of its perceived safety, it's, ahem, a little fucking unnerving to start playing big and dreaming even bigger—especially when your past is a series of fuckboys or fuckgirls. You're thinking, "But all signs are pointing to anything different than this is totally impossible." It's not easy, but you know what, **change is never, ever going to be easy.** It's going to be V. uncomfortable. Remember chapter 7's revelation: we have *got* to get comfortable with being uncomfortable. Why? Because the quality of our lives and relationships depends on it. The quality of the people we allow into our life depends on it. High quality people exist, but it's hard to find them when you're playing small and listening to the part of you that doesn't believe it. That part thinks that even if those people exist, you don't deserve them.

I know none of us thinks we are out there actively trying to find a shitty relationship, but in reality that might be exactly what we are doing. We're going into the same lackluster situations, thinking it's going to be different this time when there's nothing different about it. I thought my relationship with Mr. East Coast was going to be different and believed him when he told me he caught feelings for me. I also thought The Bartender was going to be different when he told me how special I was at two o'clock in the morning after he had a couple of beers. I let a string of meaningless words from men who knew what they were doing turn into my reality. The void caused by my trauma-driven lack of self-worth was temporarily filled up because men told me exactly what I thought I needed to hear to feel worthy.

Here's the thing: **you are one-hundred-fucking-percent worthy regardless of what anyone else thinks.** Your higher self knows you're the most amazing person on the planet who deserves all the best things in the world: epic, fulfilling love; endless zeros in your bank account; dream job; supportive friendships. You name it—you're worthy of it. You were born worthy. Your higher self gets it. On the other hand, your ego thinks where you're at now is as good as it's going to get and you've already seen the best, so there's no need to explore other options or opportunities. If you like where you're at, stay there. If you don't, switch gears, and allow yourself to connect to the part of you that desires more and believes it is there so wholeheartedly that it's like it's already your reality. That side of you is going to high tail it out of Life-sucks-ville and speed on over to Holy-shit-this-is-my-fucking-awesome-life town to revel in all the good that's coming your way.

If you're wondering how to connect to your higher self, step right up, my friend. I *also* had no fucking idea how to start. How does one start the process of connecting to all things abundance including hot, emotionally available partners? By shutting the fuck up, or, as most people like to call it: meditation. Ugh, I know. I wish there were another answer.

When I started reading about the benefits of meditation and how it helps to connect you with your higher self, your future self, and basically, you know, all the things that your dream life includes, I was like oh-my-god-that-sounds-so-great-but-I-really-don't-like-sitting-in-silence-so-there-must-be-another-way. Meditating is one of those things that's so stupidly simple and yet so stupidly hard. Why? Because it forces us to shut the hell up. And by shut the hell up, I mean stop focusing on our conscious thoughts and expand our minds to the subconscious. Yeah, I know. Seems impossible, right? I mean, there's a reason I always skipped over the pray portion of

*Eat Pray Love*, and it wasn't because I had anything against yoga or spiritual gurus. It was because the thought of meditation and mindfulness seemed so impossible that I didn't even want to bother to try. You know the saying that the things you don't want to do are usually the most important? Meditation: number one on my list.

I begrudgingly began to meditate for five minutes every day in hopes of getting answers. My meditation initially consisted of me trying not to think about anything, then thinking about everything, and then getting mad at myself for thinking things, especially for thinking I would never be a good meditator. Basically, meditating wasn't something I looked forward to. I dreaded the moment I needed to sit down. One minute felt like a half hour. You know how time can magically slow down when you're running on a treadmill? It can feel like that when you first start meditating. And sometimes it can feel like that after years of doing it. Meditation is called a practice for a reason. It's because it's something you have to consistently show up for and work on even when you really don't want to. Meditation is important because it allows us to sit down, slow down, and open ourselves and our minds to the Universe. Our thinking expands and, in turn, our consciousness grows.

When you get quiet—I mean *really* quiet—you allow the Universe (or whatever you want to call it: God, Source, Energy) to come in. Over time, meditation got easier for me. Instead of three minutes, I could meditate for six. And then ten, twenty, thirty . . . you get the picture. Instead of feeling like time had slowed down, I felt surprised by how quickly time had passed. Best of all, the benefits astonished me. Meditation significantly lowers my stress levels and helps me manage my anxiety; it's even helped me manage stressful situations better in the moment I experience them. I am always in a more calm, relaxed state following even just a few minutes of meditation. I also often feel revitalized after meditation—it's like an energy drink minus the calories! I feel more creative, inspired, mindful, and divinely connected.

Overall, I'm a happier, more confident, and grateful person. Meditation is no longer something I dread—it's something I look forward to. I've had so many epiphanies after meditating, I can't even begin to list them. I've cried, felt like I levitated, and seen my surroundings sparkle and shine as though I were sitting in a rice field in Bali. I've seen a vision of my dream life flash before my eyes and then, years later, seen it actually materialize. Meditation: it works. There are resources out there that can help you if the thought of just sitting in a room and setting a timer makes you want to scream. I personally love the app Insight Timer as it has tons of options for guided meditations, courses, sleep meditations, and more. Calm and Headspace are also great. It's 2021: there's an app for everything (besides, you know, finding your dream person. JK, there's an app for that too, and it's called Bumble—speaking from personal experience).

Before you go on your next date or even before you open a dating app, I invite you to sit down for a couple of minutes, shut up, and *listen*. See what your higher self brings to your attention. Is there more work you need to do? Is there a certain quality you need to remember you're looking for? Your higher self wants the best for you and knows it's possible. Let it drive and keep your ego in the backseat for a bit. You might come to realize that you like the change of scenery.

# Part III
# Forgiveness

(toward All the Exes She Was Unknowingly Holding on to, but Most Importantly toward Her Own Damn Self)

# Chapter 15—The Only Way to Let Go of the Person Who Did You Dirty Is the One Thing You Don't Want to Do

*When you hold resentment toward another, you are bound to that person or condition by an emotional link that is stronger than steel. Forgiveness is the only way to dissolve that link and get free.*
*—Catherine Ponder*

A few years after my vindication date with Sir L. B. (aka my real-life Scott Eastwood a la *The Longest Ride*), I heard from the modern cowboy—yet again. He slipped into my DMs to shoot his shot one final time. We were both single at that point in our lives. I had finally gone through my process of reflections and acknowledgements, and I had begun to dip my tippy toes in the world of woo-woo. I was a new-ish woman, and I had finally gotten over the boatload of stuff that had been holding me back. When you get to this point in your own journey, trust me, it's going to feel damn good to feel like *yourself* again—the self that deserves a V. amazing relationship. So, I did the whole to-go-or-not-to-go thing again and decided I'd give him a third chance. I was genuinely curious to find out what the Universe had in store.

After a two-hour phone call that seemed to last five minutes, several FaceTimes, and tons of witty back-and-forth banter, we agreed we should meet to see if the chemistry was still there between us in real life all these years and relationships later. It wasn't quite as easy as meeting up for a random Taco Tuesday though because we lived in different (albeit neighboring) states. I really enjoyed having him back in my life. Sir L. B. had always been so easy to talk to—a real conversationalist—whether it be about big dreams and adventures, or just the day-to-day stuff. Beyond being able to carry on a conversation and put up with my unique sense of humor, he remained the blue-eyed boy that stole my twenty-something heart. While he had changed in some ways, those eyes that first took me by surprise that evening at the country bar most certainly had *not*.

What I came to realize was the vindication I felt after our previous second chance wasn't vindication at all. When we went on that second chance date by the sea, my walls were still up. Subconsciously, I viewed him as the exact same fuckboy who strung me along years prior. Although I had agreed to see him again, there was no genuine second chance about it. If I'm being perfectly honest, I wanted to hurt him as much as he hurt me because, in my mind, he was the same guy who broke my young heart. Yet, while he was the same physical person (obviously), he *had* grown up, and he *had* changed. He was ready for a relationship and wanted me to be the person on the other side. Our chemistry and connection were never the issue—it was the timing. I was ready when he totally wasn't, and when he was ready, I totally wasn't.

I had been holding on to this resentment for years, like another fucked-up badge of honor symbolizing that he had done me wrong. I didn't deserve that treatment so shame on him for being such a jerk. While that definitely was true at the time and there's no excuse for what he did, there was also no excuse for me to be thinking about a relationship from that far back and carrying that pain with me for so long. How often do we hold on to resentment, anger, and hurt simply because we want an acknowledgement from the other party that they messed up and hurt us? I think it's because it makes us feel like we've somehow come out on top. It shows we didn't deserve what happened to us and that we're "better." This isn't about deserving something or not; it's about understanding that what happened, happened, and instead of wallowing in some sort of faux vindication, we really need to revel in the future and all that it can be.

I'm afraid bad timing got in the way of Sir L. B. and me for the third and final time. Every time we made plans to see each other, the plans got cancelled for one reason or another. I know I might sound like a broken record here, but the Universe is always conspiring in your favor; what I didn't realize at the time was that the Universe had someone perfect for me—someone better than the modern cowboy just around the corner. Perhaps it was a test to see if I was finally ready for the right thing and able to, you know, *know* it when it was staring back at me. We'll get to *that* later. First, I want to address the one thing I really needed to do in order to stop attracting fuckboys into my world. Unfortunately, the one thing I needed to do was the one thing I didn't want to do: **forgive.**

In order to fully let go of all the men who did me dirty along the way, I had to *honestly* forgive them. Otherwise, I would hold on to resentment, anger, and relationships that were no longer serving me. I was walking around with a ball and chain, weighed down by the fuckboys of my past, desperately trying to wade into the calm waters of emotionally available men. Angry and resentful were *not* qualities the top-notch fellows I wanted to meet were looking for. I know—the men of my past may not deserve my forgiveness, but I sure as hell deserve some freakin' peace of mind.

Forgiveness is not something that comes easily to many of us. Forgiving someone who doesn't think they did anything wrong is V. hard because we want them to acknowledge that they did something wrong. We want them to admit it because we think it will validate our pain. Here's the truth: **the only person you need to validate your pain is yourself.** Did that person hurt you? Yes. Did you deserve it? No, you most certainly did not. Do you deserve to move on and live your happiest life with your dream partner? Yes, you most certainly do. Instead of waiting for an apology you'll probably never get, it's time to put yourself out of this metaphorical misery, forgive, and move the fuck on.

This is not exactly a fun part of the process. When I had to think about The Hawaiian, The Freshman Fuckboy, Mr. East Coast, my grandfather, and other guys who, lucky for them, aren't mentioned in this book, the last thing I wanted to do was forgive them. Key their car, send them poop in the mail, and wish they would fall down the stairs were much closer to what I had in mind. So, I had to continually remind myself that in order to *truly* let them—and the pain they caused—go, I had to face all the crappy details of what happened. I had to say, and *mean*, "I forgive you." No phone calls were made. No texts were sent. This was purely between me, them (metaphorically), and the Universe. I honestly forgave them for every single thing they did. I forgave them so I could be at peace.

I forgave them for *me* because *I* deserved to be free. *I* didn't deserve to live my life with crippling resentment, shackled to a bitter past.

While forgiveness is crazy hard (especially when we forgive someone who traumatized us), it is one of the most liberating and empowering acts. Forgiveness is liberating because you are freeing yourself from the past and all the bad feelings associated with it. You're tossing it into a huge fire and walking away in slow motion like in a Hollywood film. You've conquered the villain and are on your way to do other badass things. You're no longer stuck in the prison of your past—a past that was eating away at your ability to live a truly fulfilling life and, you know, have a truly fulfilling, epic relationship.

There's nothing more empowering than taking back power from a person you had unknowingly been giving it to for years. Think about it: if you haven't fully forgiven someone who wronged you, they remain in your life and consciousness. You are letting them have control over your future instead of saying, "You know what? I don't want you here, and you don't deserve a second longer of my precious time." So, you release it all. You forgive them. Boom! The power is all back in your hands. It's empowering because you accomplish something that seems impossible, but you do it anyway because you know it is the *only* way to the other side.

The best part of this forgiveness thing? You will be one step closer to meeting your forever person. When you are able to fully free yourself through forgiveness, you will be able to focus on the future with a clear mind and heart. You're also going to feel a hell of a lot freer when you're a metaphorical two hundred pounds lighter. No longer will you be holding on to resentment—instead you'll be happy and at peace. Doesn't that sound *way* better? As a person who crossed over to the other side, I can confirm the grass is much greener over here. Plus, there's one thing the person of your dreams is going to really like: the fact that you're not still royally pissed at your ex and you don't react with a whole stinkin' pile of resentment when their name comes up. Of course, you're not going to be like, "Oh, Alex—he's such a wonderful guy even though he cheated on me with my best friend Lisa!" You'll just casually say, "Yeah, I'm so glad that relationship didn't work out because it ultimately led me to you." You're not going to be so angry all the time. No one likes someone who is angry all the time (not even fuckboys, although in my experience they'll deal with it for a solid blowie).

If you think you aren't angry, imagine your mom or another family member brings up one of your past crappy relationships at Thanksgiving dinner. While I hope this never happens to you, if in some crazy twist of events it does and you have really worked on this whole forgiveness thing, you won't turn beet red, flames won't come out of your ears, and you won't yell at your mom (or whomever) for bringing *that* up during a family function. Alternatively, if you decide to hold on to the past and stay mad, you might pull a whole Teresa Giudice versus Danielle Staub move a la *The Real Housewives of New Jersey.* Holiday dinners with your family are stressful enough—forgive, *especially* if they don't deserve it. This is about you—not them.

Anoint yourself with your own vindication: you forgave the person who wronged you. You deserve all the freedom and happiness in the world, despite what happened to you or who screwed you over. I discovered that some of the boys who wronged me did finally grow up and became the men I hoped they would. You too might find that people change. That doesn't mean you should prance into their arms and give them another shot at love (case in point, The Bartender), but it *does* mean that you can be happy for them because they've been working on themselves in the same way you've been working on yourself. Ultimately, each one of us is responsible for our own personal growth. The only person you can change and heal is yourself, no matter how much you might wish otherwise.

Of course, sometimes the one who wronged you won't ever change. Perhaps the not-so-ladylike gal who led you on for years on end is still playing the same tired games. Unfortunately, she's not exactly excited about the natural aging process and is manipulating her boy toys into paying for all her expensive plastic surgery—just to make herself feel better when she looks in the mirror. You aren't the one footing a V. expensive bill for someone who wouldn't do the same for you, and I'd call that a win. Maybe your ex is now a fifty-eight-year-old man still up to his fuckboy ways, buying Corvettes, and preying on twenty-three-year-olds. He'll be breaking hearts until he's incapable because Viagra just doesn't do the trick any longer. Am I the one buying him Viagra at Walgreens on a Friday night? Nope, I'm not. Now *that's* something to be V. thankful for. The good news with forgiveness is that you will no longer care. You don't have to let it cross your precious mind. If it does, you can let out a little giggle, thank the Universe for pushing you in a better direction, and move on knowing that you are one step closer to the epic relationship (and life) of your dreams. Doesn't that sound, you know, *dreamy?*

# Chapter 16—
# You Have Done Some Crazy Shit: Forgive Yourself Anyway

*You cannot travel back in time to fix your mistakes, but you can learn from them and forgive yourself for not knowing better.*
*—Leon Brown*

I'll never forget the day after my life-altering meltdown slash epiphany. You know, that not-so-wonderful moment referenced at the beginning of this very book? I had gone to sleep, still V. angry but oddly semi at peace, determined to wake up the next morning as if it would be the first day of the rest of my life. You know—a brand new chapter: all sparkling, crisp, and ready for any challenges that might come my way. Instead of waking up refreshed and revitalized, ready to tackle the journey to this new me, I woke up with puffy eyes, a cheap wine hangover, and the crippling realization I had no idea what the hell I was going to do. That's the reality about new chapters—there's no step-by-step process for how to change your life. The only way to change your life? By . . . changing. Revolutionary, I know.

I was tucked away in bed, avoiding getting out from under the wrinkled covers and finally getting this should-be-poignant day started because, um, I had no clue where to begin. Then *the thoughts* started pouring like Arizona monsoons in July.

How could you be so stupid and fall for the guy who had no interest in anything other than sleeping with you?

Why can't you just learn from your mistakes?

There's a twenty-three-year-old with two successful multi-million-dollar businesses and a huge book deal, and you can barely make rent every month. What's wrong with you?

Why did you eat that takeout last night instead of a salad? You're never going to have the body you want if you keep this up . . .

A variety of other very self-respecting (not) thoughts followed—just what you want right when you're getting your day started. Seriously, the number of Regina George-like thoughts filling my brain was quite intense for someone who finally made the decision to become a better version of herself. I was so mad at myself and I couldn't justify what I had done, yet again. Thankfully, I didn't spiral back into a rosé and pizza-fueled oblivion (although, frankly, I was V. close). I realized that if I was ever going to make a serious change in my life and experiences, I had to make a serious change in my reaction to the inevitable mistakes I would make. I had to forgive *myself.*

If you think forgiving someone who did you dirty is tough, forgiving yourself is the equivalent of becoming a Sports Illustrated cover model when you have:

a) never worn a bikini

and

b) never taken a picture of yourself.

Forgiving yourself, albeit ridiculously difficult to do, is *essential* to move forward and truly change your life.

You know what was one of the biggest things I hadn't forgiven myself for? What happened in Hawaii fourteen years earlier. Not being able to forgive myself for having my virginity taken without my consent is something I understand may seem counter-intuitive, but if you've experienced Trauma, you might often think about how it was somehow your fault or that you could have avoided it. I was so stuck on having made poor decisions—drinking when I shouldn't have and putting myself in a situation that wasn't safe or even remotely smart.

I couldn't come to terms with the fact that while Hawaii, along with my childhood and freshman year of college, were extremely unfortunate situations that no one could have predicted, they were *not* my fault. It was, however, my fault for letting them affect me for as long as they did. I needed to accept the fact that I could never travel back in time to change my decision that evening in order to somehow miraculously "fix" myself in present day or alter all of the mistakes I made as a result. **We cannot control what happens to us.** We *can* control how we react to what happens to us, despite how seemingly ridiculous slash impossible it may seem. As the saying goes, "hurt people hurt people." While I certainly hurt a lot of people in the aftermath, the person I was unintentionally hurting the most was myself.

By forgiving yourself, you must acknowledge what happened. You've got to face the damn thing head on. You must look at the worst decisions you have made or things you have done and say to yourself, "It's okay!" Remember, mistakes can lead to miraculous breakthroughs. Just because you're forgiving yourself though, it doesn't release you from being accountable for some things that might have happened. For example, with Mr. East Coast, I had to own the fact that I got on the plane and had sex with a guy I had never met before. I did that. It was *my* choice. It was also my choice to allow myself to fall for someone who was dressed in nothing but a V. large red flag. But in acknowledging that fact, owning it for what it was, and forgiving myself for messing up, I was able to finally let go. I was able to release the shame and guilt I felt for being V. reckless with my heart.

Forgiving yourself is the hardest act of forgiveness because you're essentially on a Disneyland ride that revisits all of your life's not-so-silver-screen-worthy moments, coupled with a song in the background that will be stuck in your head until the end of the day, if not the rest of the week. For me, the ride started with blurry visions of my grandfather's immoral and inappropriate behavior, then continued on to getting raped in Hawaii and at college, toured through falling for a carless bartender and an emotionally unavailable cowboy, not being vulnerable with a really great DJ, pretending to be Katniss Everdeen for someone when the thought of being out in nature made my skin crawl, and ended with the anti-blowout with the P.E. teacher from the Northeast. (There were a lot of other scenes on my personal reflection Disneyland ride, but for the sake of your time and my sanity, I decided not to list them all.) Let's just say this ride isn't exactly something you're going to be excited to drop a couple of Benjamins for like you might at the actual "happiest place on earth."

Facing these moments is not a fun ride. Barf bags are in the front compartment because it's not pretty or easy, and you'll want to scream at the poor attendant the whole time about how much you need to get off. Do not, under any circumstances, get off the damn ride. Even if you're screaming your head off on a rollercoaster, you wouldn't unstrap yourself and jump out because, well, you'd probably die. While the metaphorical ride doesn't have *that* kind of serious consequence, you will be met with a less than ideal fate. If you get off, you'll continue to go about your life, head in the sand, pretending like you aren't mad at yourself when you're actually one of your least favorite people. You're not going to free yourself from what's weighing you down. You can't break up with yourself, and you can't divorce yourself from the stuff you aren't so proud of. You have got to face the music, own any part you played, work through all the emotions that come up, and finally say, "You know what? I forgive myself anyway."

When I got off the ride, I felt like I had been punched in the gut by Ronda Rousey at least fifteen thousand times in a row. *It hurt.* I felt an overwhelming sense of shame for the way I had acted over the years, even though I acted that way because of the shitty things that happened to me. I'm not giving all of the ownership of this to being abused and raped, but these were horrifying things to go through, and I did not deserve them. Nor did I know that they would affect me so deeply. Maya Angelou, poet, activist, and my answer to the question, "Which person—alive or dead—would you most like to have lunch with?" said, "Forgive yourself for not knowing what you didn't know before you learned it." How often do we punish ourselves for things we did when we were so unaware? Sure, it doesn't make bad behavior or lashing out okay. It does mean that we should extend ourselves grace for not knowing what we didn't know. Ultimately, I was able to recognize that these horrific things happened, I was deeply affected by them (rightfully so), and I was trying to move on even though I didn't know *how* to move on. I made a lot of mistakes. I'm going to continue to make a lot of mistakes. Do you want to know why it's okay to make mistakes? Because you and I are human, and *all* humans make mistakes. We are not, and will never, ever be perfect (including Beyoncé—although I will admit, it sometimes seems like she is pretty damn close to perfection).

You're going to have to commit to the act of forgiving yourself for the rest of your life. It's unfortunately not a one-time thing. I realized that even after I experienced a life-changing spiritual awakening, met the person of my dreams, and started my dream career, I was still going to fall on my face and make some epic mistakes sometimes. I decided I could either fall back into the feelings of shame and guilt *or* learn to accept my mistakes, own them, and forgive myself because I am a crazy bitch who doesn't always get it right. The important thing is to understand the lesson I needed to learn as a result.

**Forgiving yourself is where the real freedom lies.** When you're able to epically fuck up, face that failure as if your life depends on it, own the fact that you were a hot mess, and say, "You know what, you really fucked shit up, but I love and forgive you anyway," that's when the real magic happens. Why? Because you have mastered the one thing all happy, successful human beings do: they don't let mistakes prevent them from moving forward and continuing to be happy and successful people who will continue to make dozens of mistakes. When you forgive yourself, you are performing an incredible act of self-love. Who is the one person you can't break up with and should love fiercely, day in and day out, mistakes included? You.

Do you want to be exactly where you are today one year from now? Do you want to be in the same miserable relationship or single and only going on dates with emotionally unavailable people or people who have zero resemblance to what you're looking for? Assuming the answer to that is a resounding "HELL NO!" I invite you to take a hard look at where you might not be letting yourself off the hook, especially with regard to matters of the heart. Are you mad that you stayed in the abusive relationship for too long? Are you angry that most of your friends are happily engaged or married but your only engagement is with Ben & Jerry's on Saturday night? Are you fucking livid that your ex-boyfriend who wasn't ready to settle down after five years of you making his lunch every day just proposed to his girlfriend of three months, and she doesn't even know what meal prep means? You've gotta face it. You've got to forgive yourself for what you've done and what you've gone through.

The most interesting part of looking into what you've done and what you're holding on to is that, most of the time, you are holding on to a *story.* You're clinging to a version of events playing in your head that isn't actually the truth. For example, my immense guilt about that night in Hawaii developed as a result of the story I told myself that if I had never gone out that night or had that drink, I would have avoided what happened. Is that the truth? Who knows? I could have gone somewhere else that evening, I could have not drunk a sip of tequila, and something terrible might still have happened to me on the way home. Or, I could have knowingly lost my virginity with someone, become attached, and had my heart broken because homeboy lived in Hawaii and I was based on the mainland. Because of the story I was holding on to, I was living in a constant state of shame. When I forgave myself, that story became false. It had no connection to me. It had no meaning at all because there is no way to know the answer to "What if . . .?" Asking yourself that question will destroy your ability to fully move forward. You'll never have the answer, so you might as well say, "I forgive myself anyway. I forgive myself because I deserve to move on and be at peace. I deserve to fall in epic love with the life of my dreams."

I forgave myself to become free, and I *know* you can do it too.

# Chapter 17—
# Bad News:
# You Might Get Ghosted Again

*When someone tells me "no," it doesn't mean I can't do it, it simply means I can't do it with them.*
*—Karen E. Quinones Miller*

Before one of my first dates post breakthrough, after I had not only acknowledged some of my not-so-appealing habits, but also had truly forgiven myself along with the men who had done me wrong, I was *excited.* I felt different, as if I had been liberated from my past self who had been constantly held back. I was Glennon Doyle Untamed. I was Mikaela version 2.0, sparkling new and just out of the she-finally-kinda-got-her-shit-together shop. As I dabbed on my concealer, filled in my brows, and took a sip of wine (just a small one to calm the nerves, I promise), I felt *confident.* I knew what I was looking for and what I deserved. I also was hellbent on keeping my pants on, even if homeboy was an Italian prince looking to find his charmingly sarcastic princess. This was it: the date I had been waiting for. I just *knew* it in my bones.

Flash forward a few hours to when I found myself face to face with a guy semi-politely letting me know he was leaving our date before the entrees had been served. Apparently, the sparkling new version of me was V. bad at first dates. Honestly, I would have preferred to be ghosted over this. Left with the bill and a gigantic pile of what-the-hell-just-happened, I found my ego stepping up to bat, reminding me of all the tired, old stories I once so firmly believed. Truthfully, my ego probably noticed all the hard work I was doing and was like, "Wait, what? What about me? Where are we going? Let's stay with the fuckboys because we know how that's gonna end!" I'm sure it was elated to find me with someone who was, if not a fuckboy, certainly less than a gentleman and who decided to cut things short on our first dinner date. Hey, when you know, you know, and apparently homeboy knew I wasn't his style. Lesson number one when you start doing all this work: your ego is probably going to try V. hard to keep you right back where you started.

I had two choices: I could let my ego take the wheel, go home, and drown my sorrows in wine and cheese while watching whatever Nicholas Sparks movie was on Netflix; or, I could decide to have a good night instead because that's what I had intended all along. It can take a long time to get ready for a night out on the town; I did my hair, I did my makeup, I got a spray tan. Beauty isn't cheap, and this time I wasn't about to waste it. Despite my slightly burned sense of self, I decided I might as well go out on the Las Vegas Strip by myself and have some fun (while I don't advise going out by yourself in Las Vegas, I did happen to live there and knew a few people where I was going).

Despite a date cut drastically short for reasons unbeknownst to me, I ended up having a spectacularly magical evening. It was straight out of a Mary Kate and Ashley movie a la 1999. That night, I met a V. famous DJ who not only taught me how to play craps in a crowded casino, but also offered to take me in his private helicopter to a music festival the following day. (Do I have a thing for DJs? All signs point to yes.) I'm very upset to report that I declined his invitation for reasons I can't even remember. Hell, even my husband wonders why I didn't go. The good news is I still sort of remember how to play craps, and I have a cool story to tell my kids someday when they're over the age of fifty-five.

While I clearly had learned some lessons (like keeping my pants on for a famous DJ), what helped me avoid my habitual derailment that evening boiled down to three concepts:

a) the importance of forgiving someone who doesn't think they did anything wrong;

b) keeping a positive attitude even though no one would have blamed me for being negative;

and

c) **any obstacle can be an opportunity for success.**

Sometimes, it can be easier to forgive someone who did something to you *in the past* because you've had time to forget some of the details. Of course, this isn't always the case, but generally speaking, if you've been holding on to something bad for a while, you normally want to let it go because you know how bad it feels to keep hanging on to it. *In the moment* someone does something to hurt you, most of the time you don't immediately think about forgiving them because you are understandably blindsided, angry, and hurt. It makes it worse when the person doesn't believe they did anything wrong in the first place. If someone hurts you, you can either forgive them or hold on to the negative feelings *until you forgive them.*

The feelings will be there until you decide to let them go. That is how you free yourself of the negative emotions you felt when you were hurt.

In the case of the not-so-gentlemanly fellow who wished me unwell mid first date, I could have easily been wildly angry and confused. I could have held on to those emotions throughout the evening and ranted about it the next morning at brunch. While, of course, it's essential to address and acknowledge how you're feeling (remember: you are the only person you need to validate your emotions), it's not great to feel upset for a prolonged amount of time. I made the decision to immediately face what happened (a guy left me by myself, in a crowded restaurant, with two filets coming shortly to the table for two turned table for one), say, "Well that guy could have handled that better and has some odd jerk-like tendencies," and believe I deserved way better. I did not deserve to feel unworthy or angry on what could still be a great evening. I forgave him, wished him well, hoped that he would heal whatever was his problem, and moved on. Then, I ordered some tequila, ate the delightful filet, and paid the bill like any grown-ass woman should. Between you and me, the waiter was certainly confused.

The waiter was confused because he knew exactly what had happened (the poor guy had practically witnessed it) and probably expected me to burst into tears or rush out of the restaurant without paying. I'm not saying I didn't want to initially do those things, but the reality is life is always going to throw us curveballs. While curveballs are never enjoyable, they do make things a bit more interesting. For me, my internal strength came from knowing that I had a lot to offer and if I could get through my childhood, Hawaii, and my college experience, I could *absolutely* get through this.

Think about how far you've come and what you've been through. Sure, it wasn't easy or fun—but talk about *resilience*. **Resilience is sexy.** You know what sexy and resilient people deserve? Epic, fulfilling, and life-altering love. That *is* out there for you, but you need to work on staying positive and happy. Of course, no one can be positive and happy 100% of the time. But what if you tried to increase your percentage of positivity—even just 1%? Keeping a positive outlook despite a tumultuous dating landscape will help keep you sane. The reality is this: ghosting and less-than-ideal first dates are inevitable. If there were a way to escape them, I assure you it would have already been readily available on a black market somewhere.

When you have gone through and reflected on your own love life, acknowledged all the things, and worked on forgiveness, there is no guarantee that your ideal mate will be the first person you run into or swipe right on Hinge. However, if you focus on staying positive despite the inevitable bumps along the way, you might start to notice how the Universe continues to be on your side. Take it from the girl who learned craps from a famous DJ when she was *this* close to running to Total Wine & More: **the Universe is always working in your favor.**

What if Ted from Tinder never ghosted you after three weeks of cheeky back and forth? Well, you might have found out that Ted is actually Ted Bundy 2.0, and I'm pretty sure that's not anyone's ideal mate. While ghosting is honestly one of the worst parts about dating these days, it's unfortunately not going away anytime soon.

Someone who ghosts a person they have been involved with is likely a V. hurt person who has V. poor communication skills. Ghosting can occur when person A decides that person B isn't the right person for them and instead of saying, "Hey, I just don't really see this working between us" they take the easy way out and just stop communicating with person B altogether. While it's extremely annoying, it's also a sign from the Universe that that person probably isn't your forever person. When you stay mad about being ghosted, you're giving away all your power to someone who doesn't think you are worth enough to communicate they are no longer interested. Does that type of human sound like someone you want to pursue further? More importantly, do you want them to have power over your feelings?

Let me be clear: I am not dismissing how awful it feels to be ghosted. It sucks. You know yourself better than anyone else, and you know what you need—whether it's a break from dating altogether, a good cry, or a boxing class where you can picture someone's face on the bag. You can't ignore your emotions and suddenly feel immense happiness and radiate positivity. If you ignore how you're *actually* feeling, it's going to have the opposite effect of the primary goal: to stop feeling like that. So, feel the feels and accept them so you can face the sunshine once more. The more you do this, the quicker you will find yourself overcoming any negative emotions that inevitably come up (trust me, twenty-five-year-old me would have run out of that steakhouse and hid under her covers for a few weeks if a guy left her mid date).

Instead of staying cranky when someone ghosts you, there are two better options:

Option A: You can call the person out, let them know that not only was ghosting you a huge fucking mistake because you have a lot to offer, but also that you hope they do better for someone else because ghosting is V. immature, and you don't have any time for that.

Option B: You can acknowledge that you've been ghosted and thank the heavens above you didn't waste any more of your precious time on a person who was incapable of effectively communicating their feelings.

If you choose option A, don't approach it with an agenda. Don't choose option A because your ego wants validation that what happened was wrong and/or you want to be acknowledged. Chances are you're not going to get a response. This is not about the response. It's about loving yourself and thinking so highly of yourself that you feel you should inform the ghoster that you deserve better, and they should do better next time if they're interested in a real relationship with an awesome person. Think of it as a mini act of self-love. Ghosting has unfortunately become common. That doesn't mean you have to accept it.

Option B doesn't mean you're validating ghosting as a proper means of ending an interaction. If you decide on this route, it should be because you don't want to waste an ounce more of your precious energy on a person who is clearly not on your level. You understand that this obstacle was nothing more than another tiny pothole on your journey to finding forever. You're okay with that because forever isn't going to end with an unanswered text.

Whichever option you choose, you're one step further on the

path to epic love. The next part of our journey together will be—for the most part—a lot more fun than taking a trip down memory lane and acknowledging all the stuff about yourself you need to change. While it started as a bumpy ride, the rest of our time together will be kind of like driving on a (mostly) smooth road, hair flowing in the breeze, with someone in the passenger seat guiding you to your final destination. There will be times when you will need an enormous amount of faith and trust in your co-pilot, but I assure you, this is the fastest way to get to where you want to be. The good news? You've had the keys to this car for a long time and your co-pilot knows the path of least resistance.

# Part IV
# Commitment

(to All This Crazy, Not-So-Woo-Wooey-after-All Behavior That Actually Fucking Works)

# Chapter 18—
# Every Bad Date Is One Date Closer to Forever

*Keep your face towards the sunshine—and shadows will fall behind you.*
*—Walt Whitman*

There are good dates and bad dates. And then there are dates where you find yourself out to dinner with a married man. Before you get up in arms thinking I finally lost my marbles and turned into a homewrecker, there was zero indication said homeboy was married because everything about him suggested he was single. For instance, there was the noticeable lack of a wedding ring on his finger, and his phone wasn't dinging every five minutes.

I met *The Doctor* in the middle of a crowded San Diego bar during college football season. Among the angry roars of the rowdy bar-goers, my best friend met him first. She thought we'd be a fantastic fit, ~~called~~ yelled at me to come over from the other side of the bar, and introduced me to a very handsome, intelligent, and witty guy who just so happened to be an actual doctor (of the PhD variety). We hit it off immediately when I joked about my BFF having scurvy as we watched her squeeze ten thousand limes into her tequila soda, and he offered me a courtesy laugh as if I were a stand-up comedian filming a Netflix special. Obviously, the fact that he was ridiculously good looking didn't hurt either. The booze flowed like the Mississippi River, and we exchanged phone numbers as drunk people at a bar often do. To be honest, I didn't think much of it, but he seemed like a guy I'd like to get to know. Also, tequila. When will I ever learn that tequila is never the beginning of something amazing?

He *called* me the next morning. Yes, he picked up a phone, called me, and left me a voicemail. Honestly, who answers the phone these days (even if they do recognize the number)? Please, just send a freakin' text. I'll answer the phone for a few select people and *that* still gives me an enormous amount of anxiety. Anyway, said voicemail consisted of a formal invitation to accompany him on a date. I obliged and a few days later, I found myself giving Dr. Hottie a hug outside of a popular local spot.

I have no idea what I expected, but it certainly was not that I would have one of *the* best first dates of my life. We closed the place down—I didn't realize that was the case until I took a breath, looked around, and noticed we were the last people in the place (with the exception of the irritated, yet I'm-still-smiling-because-I-really-need-this-tip waitress who was politely washing tables she had probably already cleaned three times). We quickly left (he paid), and he walked me to my car. The attraction between us was palpable. The inevitable first kiss was about to happen. Just when I thought he was about to go for it, he sighed heavily and let me know there was something he needed to tell me. Really? *Now?* My mind began to race.

Kids? Okay, I'd be fine with that.

Divorced? Well, as long as his ex-wife didn't divorce him because he did something horrible, that wouldn't bother me.

Serious medical condition and he only has two months to live? Hmm . . . I suppose it could be an amazing two months?

Unfortunately, I was way off. Light-years off. It was at that moment that Dr. You've-Gotta-Be-Fucking-Kidding-Me let me know he was, in fact, *happily married!* His wife not only knew about me (and the date) but had been at the bar where we met, had picked me out, and was interested in an open relationship. "This cannot be happening!" I silently screamed.

I can respect a couple's choice to have an open marriage because, you know, it's *their* relationship. Waiting until the end of an amazing first date to disclose that information to an unwitting third party probably isn't the best way to go about it. If you're wondering how our date ended after the surprise of the century, I slapped that asshole across the face (not one of my finer moments), got in my car, and sped away. I never saw him again, although he did reach out to me on multiple occasions begging for another chance. I did not entertain the idea.

Unfortunately, **bad dates are inevitable.** We are *all* going to go on some epically shitty dates. It might not be as shitty as finding out the person across the table from you is already spoken for, but bad dates come in all shapes and sizes—kind of like penises and vaginas. It's really easy to get fed up when you're on a date that you thought would be different from the rest because of your effortless banter on Bumble, but instead it goes awry. It's easy to want to throw in the towel, especially if you've been on a string of crappy dates over the past few months, years, or even decades. That said, what if you were able to view a bad date as a good thing? I know—bad dates are bad and there's no way they could ever be good. But, hear me out: **every bad date is one date closer to your last first date ever.** Really, what is more exciting than that (besides waiting for the newest *Real Housewives* reunion with Andy Cohen)?

I promise I won't get too philosophical on you, but there is an ancient Greek philosophy called stoicism that can help you turn a shitty date to your advantage. One of the core tenets of this practice is that one should endure pain or adversity with resilience. Basically, you don't let trials and tribulations—of the big or small variety—stop you from your main objective. Sometimes you have to focus on the only thing you can fully control: yourself. Staying positive despite a string of unfortunate events shows that not only are you a badass who doesn't let that nonsense bring you down, but you're a badass who is learning more and more about what you *don't* want and becoming super-duper clear about what you *do* want. There are few things in our life we have total power over—how a date will go is *not* one of them—so it's important to remember that sometimes you just have to accept what you can't control and make the decision to not let it bring you down for good. Who knows? You might meet Mr. or Mrs. Forever in line at the grocery store on your way home, and you might just happen to be holding the exact same bottle of rosé. The Universe works in mysterious ways, but it certainly rewards those who aren't perpetually down in the dumps after an obstacle gets in the way.

I get it—you're not going to shout from the rooftops with glee after a horrible date (see my reaction in the last chapter). It's not going to be your initial response, especially if it's not the first, second, or thirty-seven millionth time it's happened. How many times have you caught yourself wondering some iteration of the following: How did [insert name here] meet their match on Tinder and get engaged six months later when I'm just as cool and funny and attractive? It's frustrating and tends to get worse as we cross over decades when many of our friends have moved on to families and white picket fences. Keep in mind chapter 10's revelation: everyone is on their own timeline. Comparison will always make you unhappy so you might as well, you know, *not* compare yourself to anyone but yourself. While it's more than okay to be initially upset (you must honor your feelings, for better or for worse), it's not okay to let it ruin your entire day, week, year, etc. I've never heard about a date that ruined someone's entire year (although I'm fairly confident there's a mega-heartbreaker out there who could make it happen).

Let yourself feel whatever it is, face it, and then remind yourself that **you're a fucking catch.** This person (while they did waste a bit of your time) was thankfully only part of your life for a few hours. You are now one date closer to the miraculous feeling of "Oh! So *this* is what it feels like to be treated well by an emotionally available human." Trust me on this one: *that* date is going to knock your socks off (even if you aren't wearing any).

If me simply requesting your trust isn't going to do it for you, let me offer another point of view that might make more sense. If you were on a date with someone who was super negative, jaded, and all around seemingly unhappy, would you want to go out with that person again? My guess is probably not. Alternatively, what if you went out on a date with a person who was totally engaging, upbeat, compelling, and genuinely interested in what you had to say? Would you want to see that person again? I know I would, especially if said person made my panties do a little dance.

The same goes for the other side! If you're jaded from all your bad dates and have won a Golden Globe for your performance as Debby Downer, the person sitting across from you probably won't be keen on seeing you again. It's more likely they'll be desperately thinking of a plan to escape from your negative vibe. While it is okay to feel angry, sad, or whatever it is you're feeling, it is *not* okay to walk around, especially on a date, projecting your jadedness like nobody's business. I know sometimes you don't think you're giving off those vibes on a first date but honestly, most of us—including yours truly—have been guilty of doing just that.

Alternatively, let's consider a scenario where you adopt the notion that every bad date is one date closer to epic love, nothing can get you down forever, and you love yourself because you're you and you deserve an amazing relationship. The party on the other side of the table is going to pick up what you're putting down. That positive energy will be circulating out and about. You'll appear not only vibrant and intriguing, but also like someone they want to be around more because your vibe makes them feel better. People want to be around people who make them feel better. You'll know if you're doing a good job at this because people *will* want to be around you more. You'll be raising the collective vibe! If you're wondering what the hell a vibe even is or what role it plays in the romance department, we'll dive into that in chapter 21.

You have a big decision to make here because as you get older, dating *doesn't* miraculously get any easier. The pool might get smaller, you're going to get pickier (as you learn what you do and do not want), and everyone around you is going to have an opinion about it. You can either:

a) bitch and moan about how crappy dating is, how it's just a sea of losers, and that you have terrible taste in partners

or

b) dust off your shoulders, remind yourself that if dating were easy, everyone would have already found their forever person, and go on every date with an open mind (and open heart) believing that it's one date closer to the last first date of your life.

The moment I decided to switch from the *a* mentality to the *b* (for better) option and committed to this mindset, dating became much less of a drag and more of a tool I could use to find the man of my dreams. I went on a *lot* of bad dates, mediocre dates, and great dates before I had my last first date (which just so happened to be the best first date of my life). I didn't let any of those not-so-awesome dates deter me from my new way of thinking because I *committed* to the belief it was all part of the journey to lead me to exactly what I wanted. As usual, the Universe delivered.

So, what's it going to be: *a* or *b*? I think you know which direction I'm trying to nudge you toward.

# Chapter 19—
# If You Want an Ass Like JLo, You Gotta Do Some Squats

*Even the smallest shift in perspective can bring about the greatest healing.*
*—Joshua Kai*

There comes an unfortunate moment in everyone's life when they realize a steady diet of cheese, carbohydrates, and red wine is no longer going to cut it. Metabolism is a bitch, huh? I'll never forget the moment I came to the horrifying conclusion I could no longer consume my three favorite (aforementioned) food groups and kind-of-sort-of partake in half-assed workouts and yoga classes without that behavior having an undesirable effect on my waistline. *All* bodies are beautiful, and it's important to love yourself regardless of your clothing size; however, it is important for me to not only look good, but also *feel* good and healthy. And it doesn't feel too good to be huffing and puffing through a beginner's yoga class after consuming approximately three pounds of cheese and two bottles of wine the night before.

In an effort to tighten things up and not feel like I was going to pass out two minutes into a workout class, I decided to venture into the wonderful virtual world we call YouTube to find some workouts to try in the comfort of my own home. It was there, in my living room, that I met Pamela Reif. My goal of not passing out two minutes in was short-lived because I honestly thought I was going to die forty seconds in when it felt like I had been holding a plank for over ten minutes. Seriously, time stands still when you're doing a plank—it's science. Pamela Reif is a strikingly gorgeous twenty something who somehow creates the most difficult workout you could think of, does it herself, and doesn't appear to be in any sort of physical pain whatsoever while you're sweating your non-existent ass off, trying to catch your breath, and your heart rate is higher than your Apple Watch has seen in many moons. In short, her workouts are great for anyone who is interested in ten to thirty minutes of pain—and undeniable results.

Despite my pathetic first, second, and eighteenth appearances on my living room carpet tuning into Pamela, I slowly but surely got better. While the seventy-nine thousand squats, lunges, and planks never stopped sucking, and I wanted to stop every day, I did start to notice a difference. My waist was a little tighter, booty a little bit juicier, and, most importantly, I was like, "DAMN, GURL!" every time I walked by a mirror. While the last part is a slight exaggeration, I did start to feel a lot better about how I looked and how I *felt*. **Life is too damn short to not feel good and confident in your skin.**

Every morning when I pulled on my tattered workout clothes, I did not want to do it. Some days I had more energy than others, but collectively, I would put it off and avoid it, and then remind myself that it would help me feel amazing. In the wise words of the iconic Elle Woods, "Exercise gives you endorphins. Endorphins make you happy." While I wasn't always happy when I had to do glute bridges, burpees, and other torturous moves, I was always happy when I finished. Endorphins: they are your friend.

My commitment to exercise reaped a variety of benefits: I was no longer the queen of flab, I had a butt my husband wanted to grab in public, I enjoyed an increase in self-esteem and overall confidence in my body, I felt stronger and more powerful, and it instantly put me in a better mood. It's important to remember that commitment is key. Imagine if I showed up for that first ten minutes, first day, or first week thinking that I would have the keys to Jennifer Lopez's castle and immediately have a bangin' bod for life. It ain't gonna happen, honey! Like JLo, I had to be *committed* to showing up, sweating my ass off, even (and most importantly) when I didn't want to. Otherwise, I'd never have an ass like JLo, and honestly, who doesn't think she has a great booty?

Just like a commitment to exercise will help you get a healthier, stronger body (and the booty of your dreams), the same goes for your inside. Working on your mental health—doing the inner work—is just as important as working on your physical health. In fact, it may be more important. The benefits of inner work, like exercise, are not instantaneous. It is not as simple as thinking one nice thought about yourself and immediately feeling fully healed. It is a practice you must be committed to showing up for daily, even when you don't want to. It's a muscle that you need to strengthen. I'll spare you the visual from my first Pamela workout, but it wasn't pretty. It's also not going to be pretty when you start working on yourself either. It might feel painful and hard at first, but over time, it *will* get easier.

One of the most challenging parts about starting to work on

your inner self is becoming aware of how you talk to yourself on a regular basis. As we've come to see, the number of self-loathing and highly critical thoughts I had about myself daily were astonishing. It could have been anything from punishing myself for not raising my hand to speak in a meeting, hating how I looked in the mirror, to chastising myself if I—gasp!—made a mistake. Over and over again, I would say awful things to myself. And then, *my thoughts became my reality.*

**Everything begins in our minds.** Ev-er-y-thing. If you think you're a terrible-horrible-good-for-nothing person undeserving of love, you're going to feel terrible, horrible, and undeserving of love. When you're feeling that way, you're going to be vibrating at a pretty low frequency, and you're probably not going to attract your ideal mate who will likely be vibrating way closer to the metaphorical top. This person is going to be on Mount Everest while you're swimming with the bottom feeders in the Black Sea. All because you thought you were undeserving of love, felt that way, and brought yourself down another notch. Thoughts. Emotions. Reality. They're all connected, baby.

On the other hand, let's say you start becoming aware of any negative thoughts and *commit* to stop believing that old story. Let's say you commit to focusing on being loving to yourself, thinking compassionate thoughts, and giving yourself grace constantly *simply because you deserve it.* If you commit to this practice, you might begin to notice you're talking to yourself differently. For example, you look in the mirror and see dimples on the back of your legs or arms that aren't super defined. Perhaps you immediately go into your old mindset, hate how it looks because society puts an enormous amount of pressure on us to look perfect all the time, and rush to put on something that will cover them up. Thanks to the work you've been putting in, you catch yourself going down the rabbit hole of negativity and remind yourself of how awesome you are and how beautiful your body is. You're thankful for showing up to the workouts and love that you've become stronger. You'll automatically feel better and your vibration will rise. No longer are you swimming with the little fishes; you're surfing the waves to the shore ahead!

Your thoughts are connected to every single thing in your life—including the love department. One of my biggest struggles when I was first experimenting with mindfulness was that I could not wrap my head around coming from a place of abundance. Nothing in my life was abundant, or so I thought. I thought this way because I was operating from a place of scarcity in all areas of my life. I was so focused on what I didn't have that I didn't appreciate what I did, and I sure as hell didn't believe there were more things available for me—especially of the limitless variety.

A limiting belief system keeps you from everything you want because you're, you guessed it, limited. Unfortunately, most of the time you have zero clue you're operating from this mindset because it's what you learned V. young, and you've always thought this way. Changing the way you've thought for years isn't exactly the easiest thing in the world to do. Is it important if you want to live the life of your dreams and stop wasting your time on people who don't deserve you? Hell to the yeah! This is a commitment you must make to yourself to change. Change is never easy, but it is the only way to grow. It starts with awareness. Being able to identify your limiting beliefs is a huge step in the process. When I started researching this topic, I was like "Holy-fucking shit. This is exactly my problem!" Because I was always focused on what I didn't or thought I couldn't have, I never opened up the possibility to myself, let alone the Universe, that there was even a *chance* of anything more.

Where your thoughts sow, your reality grows. Because I didn't believe good men existed, good men did not come into my life. And, if they did exist, they sure as hell weren't interested in someone like me who was so negative all the time. I decided to dive in on the opposite side of the pool: a place of abundance. This is really hard, by the way, when you're living paycheck to paycheck, making sure your dog eats before you do, and haven't had a totally happy relationship, like, ever. I started to think about other people around me—my friends, co-workers, and even people I followed on Instagram. Why couldn't I have what they have? What was wrong with me? Lim-itting be-lief! When you come from a place of abundance, it doesn't matter what anyone else has because you know you are worthy of every single thing you want, and that there's more than enough of it to go around. Literally, it's limitless.

Often, we're stuck in a way of thinking that goes something like this: if Britney has ten million dollars, a fabulous partner, a successful career, and she vacations 366 days out of the year, that means there is ten million dollars less for the rest of us, one more great person off the market, another person to compete against career-wise, and another reason I have to work overtime at my crappy job, which I hate. This couldn't be further from the truth. **The reality is that we *all* can have it all.** There are limitless pieces of pies. In fact, there are so many pies we couldn't possibly eat them all—you just have to tap into a way of thinking that believes that to be true.

Here's another super-duper-awesome way to think about it when you see other people that make you envious: it's a sign from the Universe that you can have what they have too. Next time you come across a person who has something you really, really want, remind yourself that it's just the Universe whispering in your ear, "Psst. This is totally and completely possible for you, too."

Having an abundant mindset isn't something that happens overnight, and it's also something you have to be committed to every day, especially when things inevitably don't go your way. If you tap into this once, feel uber alive and abundant, but then two weeks later your check engine light turns on and it's a $5,000 bill, you might slip back into the mindset of the person who can't believe this has happened again, wonders where the heck the money is going to come from this time, and thinks there's no way they can figure this out . . . you get the picture. Life is going to happen, for better and for worse, and the best way to stay vibrating high is by committing to showing up and reminding yourself of abundance every damn day like your quality of life depends on it, because it *does.*

Coming from a mindset of abundance means that you don't hold on to things (like money, for example) because you're scared they will never come back. This isn't permission to spend your life savings on a Birkin bag, but it is okay to splurge on an occasional treat like a massage that makes you feel relaxed and amazing. Know that you deserve it, and don't feel guilty because that money is going to come back to you. Similarly, in the dating world, coming from a place of abundance doesn't mean there will suddenly be a mile-long line of dates outside your door vying for your love and affection. It does mean that you know your person is out there for you despite any experiences suggesting otherwise.

Easy? No.

Essential? Yes.

Remind yourself, every day, every hour, *all the fucking time*, that your thoughts are creating your reality. If you like where you are, wonderful! Keep doing the same thing and thinking the same way. If you don't like where you are or the status of your (love) life, pay attention to your negative thoughts, commit to changing them, and know that the abundance of the Universe is completely available to you for no other reason than **you deserve it.**

# Chapter 20—
# If You Think Your Life Sucks, It's Always Going to Suck

*The mind has a powerful way of attracting things that are in harmony with it, good and bad.*
*—Idowu Koyenikan*

Like most millennials, I grew up to the sounds of pop music a la *NSYNC, Backstreet Boys, and Britney Spears. While they're all still semi-relevant today, my girl Britney has always known how to drop some serious hits and has arguably one of the most interesting Instagram accounts of any celebrity out there. My personal favorite song of Ms. Brit's described my late twenties to a tee: "Toxic." After years of dating emotionally unavailable fuckboys, I entered what would turn into a nearly three-year, V. toxic relationship that honestly shouldn't have survived beyond date number two. The most unfortunate part about a toxic relationship is you don't realize how toxic it is until you're nearly in too deep.

I stayed in this relationship despite multiple bouts of infidelity, immeasurable immaturity, and some serious emotional (and sometimes physical) abuse. Friendships were lost, and family members wondered if I had actually lost my mind. I remained dedicated to working things out and operated under the mentality that this was as good as it could be, even though that was far from the truth.

I was chronically depressed and financially fucked; I felt like the only option was to stay in my realm of misery because I didn't believe there was a way out or that the outside had anything better to offer. Did any of that make sense to the people who knew me? Absolutely not.

When you find yourself in this position, wondering how you became part of a statistic, it honestly feels easier to give up rather than try to end things, move on, and be by yourself again. In my mind this was the best that was available for me. Other people could have normal relationships, but I couldn't. I mean, my past was nothing but a string of messed up relationships with messed up guys—I couldn't even envision what my life would look like without that because it was all I had ever known. Everything around me pointed to my tried and true story: this was as good as it gets *for me.*

Then, one day, I came across the book that changed my life: *You Are A Badass* by Jen Sincero. "Me? A badass?" I thought, as I looked around my empty apartment to see if anyone was watching me buy a self-help book on Amazon. There was nothing badass about me at the time—or so I thought. I was in this horrible relationship and working at a job I hated, all while living paycheck to paycheck and trying to keep it together enough so no one would ask me any questions. When the book came in the mail, I ripped open the package and dove right in, finishing it in about two days. I've re-read it about thirty-eight times, or whenever I needed a kick in the ass to be the badass I totally am. That book stirred something inside of me that had been desperately trying to get out, but that I had refused to look in the freakin' face. I was met with the harrowing reality that if I didn't change the way I thought about things, I was going to stay here for the rest of my life. That wasn't a life I was interested in living, and I venture to guess that isn't one you're interested in living either. I was acting like I was powerless in this relationship when in reality I had all the power I needed inside of me all along, and it was about damn time I took it back.

There was no way I was meant for this. I deserved a happy ending without the abuse, alcoholism, and anger that had permeated this relationship for so long. I was well overdue for something great, so I decided to end things once and for all. While it wasn't easy or uncomplicated by any stretch of the imagination, I did the damn thang. I made a commitment to myself that I deserved better and decided to believe that better *was* out there. The Universe, as we now understand, is a limitless thing. There isn't a limited number of resources available to us. While the news headlines and your Bumble messages might suggest otherwise, there isn't a finite number of emotionally available, attractive, incredible partners out there. There's a ton of them out there—we just have to believe that they exist. **If your dream partner doesn't exist in your mind, they aren't going to exist in your line of sight.**

The reality: whatever you think is possible will be possible for you. This goes for *both* ends of the spectrum. If you believe that your life is a miserable mess, your life is going to be miserable and messy. If you think that there are no good options left in this world, there won't be thousands of solid date options sliding into your DMs. If you think that you're going to be single forever, you're going to be single forever. On the flip side, if you believe that, despite your current single status, one day you're going to be in the relationship of your dreams, you could end up with that dreamy DJ. If you think your life is an incredible gift that attracts love and prosperity, you will live the American dream with loads of money and tons of amazing romantic interests all vying for your favor. If you think this is impossible, it's going to be impossible for you. As the girl who was literally bankrupt and feeling stuck in a nightmare, I assure you: it's not impossible. Unfortunately, I can't do the work for you—it lies within you, and you alone. Are you beginning to believe *you* are literally everything you have ever needed?

Being committed to a positive mindset rooted in abundance isn't something that comes naturally to someone who has been operating under a scarcity mindset for years. You might be in this situation if:

- you don't believe you can have something if someone already has it
- you are scared to give something up because you believe it will never come back to you (for example, talking yourself out of spending a lot of dough on something you really want)
- you don't feel deserving of something or someone
- the idea that you can make millions or billions of dollars doing something you love makes you roll your eyes
- you complain to your friends at brunch about how much dating sucks, how you're going to be single forever, and that all the "good ones" are taken

Those are just a few examples. A scarcity mindset is rooted in the ideas that there is not, and never will be, enough of something and that some things are impossible for you. **Newsflash: an-y-thing**

**and an-y-one is a possibility.** If your dream is to live on a yacht in the Mediterranean being served fresh oysters (one by one) by Tom Hardy, well, it can happen; but you have to believe that it is possible for you—I mean, *really* believe it, as if you're already nibbling on the delightful libido boosters with a shirtless Mad Max nearby. I'll go into the details of how to do this in the next section, but it all starts (and ends) with your mind. If you're stuck in the scarcity mindset, you're never going to get all that you desire and deserve. Just ask Matt Damon's (stunning) wife, Luciana Barroso, who met her movie star turned real-life husband one fated evening when she was waiting tables at a Miami nightclub—I'm pretty sure she wasn't coming from a place of scarcity when she locked him down.

People who have an abundant mindset *know* the world is their oyster. Imagine an all-you-can-eat-and-drink buffet of every single thing you could dream of. The entrees are constantly replenished, your drink is always full, and somehow your stomach never gets bigger. It's a Christmas freakin' miracle! Abundant thoughts look like:

- I can't wait to meet my forever person who is already on the way and looking for someone exactly like me.
- Buying this expensive thing is OK because I really want it, it's going to bring me so much happiness, and the money will flow back to me freely.
- It's okay to buy this expensive champagne because it tastes so much better than André and doesn't give me a nasty headache.
- I'm so excited to live in this beautiful apartment that lights me up like a Christmas tree and inspires me to do all the things I love doing.

Counterintuitive at first? Totally. The more you do it, the more natural it becomes. We're committing here, right?

The first step to addressing this whole scarcity situation is to, you know, acknowledge that's what's going on. Like in the beginning of the book where we walked through acknowledging adverse (dating) habits, we have to acknowledge the limiting beliefs we're letting control our thoughts. If you acknowledge that this is an area that needs improvement for you, committing to noticing these thoughts and reframing them into abundant ones is a must. We can't control our thoughts, sadly, but we can notice if a thought isn't *true.* I thought that my toxic relationship was the best I could do. Was that remotely true? What evidence suggested that it was my only destiny? When I investigated that thought, I could think of more evidence that it *wasn't* true than evidence suggesting it was.

Engaging with our thoughts and questioning their validity helps to identify the old stories we let ourselves believe. Let's say after a horrifyingly bad first date you think, "There are no good ones left!" Let's work on questioning that limiting belief. How many single people exist today? The current world population is V. high. And by high, I mean there are more than seven billion people on the planet. That's a massive number! Regardless of what your reality looks like at this very moment, if you were to focus on the fact that there are millions of eligible partners out there who are looking for someone exactly like you, it's a much more enticing thought than the idea that there are no good options left in the world. Sure, it might seem silly at first and possibly pointless depending on your previous experiences, but in all honesty, what do you have to lose here? Personally, I had nothing to lose and *everything* to gain.

Committing to this practice will—without a freaking doubt—change your life. But if you're still afraid to try it, consider this: the worst-case scenario is that you stay exactly where you are, which, coincidentally, is exactly where you'll be if you don't try this. The only difference between people who are uber successful and in happy relationships and those that aren't is that the happy people believed it was possible for them—they knew that it was available and on the way to them. It doesn't mean they're *always* successful and *always* happy, it just means that instead of letting a bump in the road (or several potholes) stop them from believing, they just believe it more deeply. The Universe has a sense of humor, which I'll discuss more in chapter 24, but ultimately, just because you actively work on an abundant mindset instead of a scarce one, it doesn't mean your life is going to be picture perfect every day.

Dedication is important because it shows an unwavering commitment to what is possible for you. And remember, ev-er-y-thing is. Seriously, I mean it. You can roll your eyes all you want, but if you want to stop messing with losers, you have to be committed to a mindset that believes there are eighteen football fields of super-hot, kind, confident, and well-mannered single people on their way to you. What would happen if you truly believed that everything you wanted was not only already on its way to you, but wanted you back? IDK about you, but I decided, "Why not?", gave it a whirl, and had a ring on my finger before I knew what I had even done. If I had played it safe and stayed in that long, drawn-out, toxic relationship, I'd have no ring, no money, and no self-respect. This one's up to you: play big or stay small?

# Chapter 21—
# The Universe Wants You to Have an Orgasm *Every* Time

*There is a truth deep down inside of you that has been waiting for you to discover it, and that truth is this: you deserve all good things life has to offer.*
*—Rhonda Byrne*

How many times have you faked something in your life? Yes, you! Did you beef up your resume in order to be considered for a certain job? Have you ever lied to impress someone you were out on a date with? Maybe you've faked not feeling well or being busy just to get out of an event you really didn't want to go to in the first place so you could curl up on your couch and watch Netflix instead. While I won't reveal whether yours truly is guilty of all of the above, there is one thing I'm not so proud of—but I have decided to share with you anyway. I, Mikaela Kostaras, am V. guilty of faking an orgasm. If I'm being honest, I'm pretty sure (before I met my husband) I faked more orgasms than I actually had. While I'm hoping I'm somewhat of an outlier here, the Internet offers several stories showing me that I'm not alone in this kinda-sorta-totally embarrassing statistic. Faking an orgasm is unfortunately way more common than it's not. While some ladies demand the Big O (I bow down to you if you're one of them), some can be V. guilty of pretending they don't have the female equivalent of blue balls. But why fake something that, quite honestly, shouldn't be faked? Most fake it for one or two (or both) reasons:

1. We think faking it will help keep the relationship happy, and therefore keep the person in our life.
2. We don't want to hurt our partner's feelings.

In the case of Mr. East Coast, I didn't get there more often than I did (on second thought, I don't think I even had one orgasm, which makes my whole meltdown that much more depressing). Did I pretend otherwise? Yes, I did. While I should have interpreted this as yet another sign that homeboy just wasn't my destiny—or even worth a fun weekend—I was hellbent on making it happen for some reason. I thought that faking having a great time in the bedroom would keep him in my life. Yes, it kept him in my life for the exact reason he shouldn't have stayed: the sex. We know sex was equivalent to love in my mind, but did the fact that I didn't even have great sex as a memory make it more bitter when things ended? One hundred percent. Here's the truth: faking an orgasm might keep the other person happy and convince them to stick around, but you're not going to be happy if you can't, you know, get there. That's also not something you deserve for the rest of time. As we learned with The Comedian, what you *do* deserve is spectacular sex *all* the time. Ironically, the Universe couldn't agree more.

As far as being afraid to hurt someone's feelings—I get that. I'm an empath to the core and feel *all* the feels of people around me. While it might not be easy to acknowledge that someone couldn't get you there, it may open an opportunity to have a deeper discussion of what *could.* Maybe you need your engine revved for a little longer, or maybe you were just crazy stressed. Having the Big O isn't just about stimulation. It's about your mind. If the person you're with is secure, they will want to get you there every single time and, if that doesn't happen, they will likely be open to your ideas. It doesn't get much more intimate than a discussion of orgasms over Sunday dinner. Pop open a nice bottle of red, and the ideas might start flowing!

While some of us might be faking something so seemingly silly as an orgasm, we shouldn't be faking anything at all—qualifications for a job or a faux illness to miss an event included. Of course, it's important to fake a smile at your boss to be appropriate, but beyond having decent manners, the Universe doesn't like anything but the whole truth (and nothing *but* the truth). The Universe also knows the truth anyway, so there's no point in hiding it. Something else that the Universe and I are both pretty damn sure of? You *can* have an orgasm every time. As I referenced before, you can have anything (I mean an-y-thing) you want. A kind-hearted, multi-billionaire who happens to be Damon Salvatore in real life, minus the whole vampire with an attitude problem thing? Yep, coming right up. A million bucks in the bank? Totally possible for you, my darling. Anything you think of, want, and/or desire, can be yours. Sounds pretty awesome, right?

But . . . there has to be a catch. Right? Nope! The girl who faked an orgasm for a guy who wasn't into her at all was able to attract epic love and meet and marry the man of her Nicholas Sparks–driven dreams just by understanding, committing to, and believing in the Universal Laws. The Universal Laws aren't something any of us has learned in school or had to pass a test at the DMV for. If I had been offered a course in them in high school, I probably would have scoffed and selected something seemingly “cooler” like fine art or photography instead, not realizing the power these laws have over, you know, *everything*. While the Law of Attraction is pretty widely known thanks to *The Secret* by Rhonda Byrne, there are other laws that are just as noteworthy. Here is a V. brief overview of these Universal Laws as presented on the website MindBodyGreen:

1. Law of Divine Oneness: everything is connected—our thoughts, actions, senses, words; a pen, a book, a person, a tree. Whatever. It's *all* connected, baby!
2. Law of Vibration: it's time to vibe up! Every single thing, though connected to everything else, is vibrating at its own level or frequency. Whether it's a tiny atom, a butterfly, a hundred year-old tortoise, a fuckboy, or a sparkling diamond, everything carries a unique vibration. Our vibrational frequency can be V. low when we're all grumpy and negative (thus attracting other grumpy, negative people). Alternatively, when we're happy, gracious, and loving every little thing, we're vibrating high. People who are on the same level are going to be drawn to each other naturally.
3. Law of Correspondence: what's happening in our reality is happening inside of us, kinda like a mirror. If our life is chaotic, we're chaotic inside. If our life is full of emotionally unavailable people, we're likely emotionally unavailable ourselves.
4. Law of Attraction: Oh, my favorite! The Law of Attraction works on the basis of the Law of Vibration, which is why it's

important to vibrate higher (as I suggested in chapter 18). This is where manifestation occurs—like attracts like. You have to focus on what you want and believe you can obtain it. Let me be clear: focus on what you *want*, not what you don't want (in other words, stop focusing on losers). Your vibration is ev-er-y-thing when it comes to making your dream life a reality. Don't worry, we dive into this in the next section.

5. Law of Inspired Action: You have to, you know, do *something*, in order to get whatever it is that you want. If you never leave your apartment, you're not going to meet the partner of your dreams. This doesn't mean that you have to be constantly go-go-going, it just means you should allow the Universe to nudge you in a direction and then take an inspired action. Inspired action comes naturally, effortlessly, and flows. Inspired action never feels forced.

6. Law of Perpetual Transmutation of Energy: everything in the Universe is constantly fluctuating. Think of a Debbie Downer: no one wants to be around one because when they are, their mood starts to, you know, go down. Alternatively, if you're around someone who is charismatic and happy, your mood might shift in a positive direction.

7. Law of Cause and Effect: if you put something out there, the energy will have a ripple effect. If you're resentful, it's going to come back to you in a way you might not enjoy. Karma can be a babe or a bitch—which one do you want heading your way?

8. Law of Compensation: your effort to do or get something is going to come back to you in a positive way—if you water a seed, it will grow into a beautiful, green plant. If you ignore it,

it'll die. Contribute to your goal. In this case, how will you contribute to the success of your (love) life?

9. Law of Relativity: comparison is the thief of joy, and beauty is in the eye of the beholder. It comes down to our perspective. If you're feeling crappy about your love life or relationship status, it's probably because you're comparing yourself to someone else. That's not going to help things, at all. If you appreciate what you *do* have, it will help you feel a ton better.

10. Law of Polarity: everything has an opposite—fuckboys versus emotionally available men, for instance. The key here is that contrast brings more clarity. If you're experiencing something bad, think of the opposite. This might help you understand a lesson you've been missing.

11. Law of Rhythm: everyone has a cycle. There will be times when we're full of energy whereas at other times it's exhausting to get out of bed. Work with it instead of fighting against it (i.e., it's okay to take a freakin' break).

12. Law of Gender: one of my other personal favorites, this is all about masculine and feminine energies. It doesn't have any thing to do with identity because we all have both within us. Our society is built on masculine energy—the hustle mentality. Finding a balance between masculine and the divine feminine, which is all about flowing, is ideal for a harmonious life. And, by the way, emotionally unavailable people are typically a result of wounded masculine or feminine energy.

Your one-way ticket to falling in epic love with your life is rooted in the understanding of these laws and how they can (and will) totally change your life. Specifically, I want to draw your attention to the all-too-well-known Law of Attraction—it isn't just some woo-woo concept that only works for spiritual gurus while the rest of us are left with crumbs in the back of the line. The Law of Attraction works for anyone and everyone, but it requires a serious commitment and an unwavering belief that whatever you want is already yours (because the Universe *will* test you).

Your commitment to this will change your life—your love life, professional life, financial life, mental life—all aspects of you and your reality. The cool part about it? It doesn't cost you a dime because the only thing you need to make it work is, you know, you.

The Law of Attraction is basically the Universe dressed up as Elle Woods in nothing but fifty shades of pink saying, "What? Like it's hard?" to anything and everything we could possibly imagine. Whether you want to manifest a partner, a marriage, a million dollars, or a partner with a million dollars who wants to marry you, you can do it. It's not as easy as thinking it, saying a quick "Hey thanks in advance!" to the Universe and the very next day, it all shows up on your doorstep. It also doesn't have to be insanely hard. We love to over complicate things for ourselves sometimes, don't we? It couldn't possibly be that easy, could it? Well, honestly, it *can*—as long as you're committed with an unwavering trust in the unknown.

I began to practice all these laws daily—particularly the Law of Attraction (while keeping my vibration in mind)—and witnessed mind-blowing outcomes. Most remarkably, I manifested the man and epic love of my dreams. I realize this might sound outlandish, but there is no other way to put it. While everyone's path looks different, everyone is capable of attracting the love they desire and deserve—including you. Since you picked up a book about how to upgrade your (love) life, I'm going to assume you'd like to see a change. Your mind can create the reality you want—down to every single detail. You are more powerful than you know, and hopefully, after the next five chapters, you'll start to understand that you've had the keys to unlock the door to ev-er-y-thing you want this whole time. The Universe will always say yes to you. Are *you* ready to say yes to you? **Are you ready to believe in the impossible?**

Before you put the book down and mindlessly scroll through social media for forty-five minutes, think about what it would *feel* like to have everything you ever wanted. I mean, everything: dream job, dream relationship, dream house, dream car, dream bank account balance—all of it. Honestly, how would it feel? My guess? It would feel pretty damn exhilarating because you would have everything you ever wanted. Some people in this world *do* have everything they ever wanted. You aren't any different from those people. You have the same organs, same neurons, and the same humanness. They just believed in the impossible, no matter what. Seriously, you don't have anything to lose—and you might be surprised at everything you gain.

# Part V
# Faith

(You Must Believe Because There Is No Other Option, except to Go Back to the Old You, Which Sounds like the Worst Idea . . . Ever)

# Chapter 22—When You Tell the Universe What You Want, It Will Deliver It to Your Apartment Complex

*Ask for what you want and be prepared to get it!*
*—Maya Angelou*

In college, I wrote and presented an unintentionally ironic speech for my public speaking class about how online dating was pointless. I had thirty slides all about how it wasn't remotely effective or useful and totally wasn't the way to meet your forever person. Besides being eighteen and not having a damn clue what was in store for me, I'm pretty sure the Universe was giggling from the back of the classroom, knowing that I'd ultimately meet my own Mr. Forever on a dating app. I don't know how many times I have to repeat this, but if you *don't* think the Universe has a sense of humor, you couldn't be further from the truth.

I avoided online dating for over a decade, unable to believe I could meet a non-fuckboy on a dating app. I had heard all the horror stories from friends and strangers alike and, for the most part, didn't have a problem meeting men on my own. As you've read, I met most of the guys I dated at bars or nightclubs. It's not impossible to encounter your modern-day Mr. Darcy meets Christian

Grey after a couple of dirty martinis, but there's a reason Hallmark movies aren't typically set in the middle of a busy speakeasy.

Of course, after a decade of fuckboys and failed relationships, I gave the good old heave-ho to my previous distaste for apps and decided to bite the bullet. I didn't have immediate luck with the apps. Case in point: the P.E. teacher—Mr. East Coast—who almost broke me. The anti-gentleman who left me with two entrees and the bill at a restaurant is another example. I've been where you are, and there's no sugar coating it: online dating is V. hard; but, if you tell the Universe what you want, there is a chance it will deliver it to your apartment complex—or at least that's what happened to me.

A few months after I told the Universe exactly what I wanted and began to believe I was going to manifest the man of my dreams, I hopped onto Bumble one night after work and got to swiping semi-mindlessly while Netflix blared in the background. I remember looking at this guy with an odd name who had semi-decent photos (seriously, who here wants to start a business helping people with their dating profiles?!) and thinking, hmm . . . he seems cute. I swiped right, sent a witty message that referenced something in his profile about a disdain for mirror selfies and wouldn't you know it, a witty message popped right back. One of the most important qualities I sought in my forever guy, besides intelligence, was the ability to understand my sense of humor, which doesn't always translate with the opposite sex. After about a week of back-and-forth banter as well as some deep conversations, he asked if he could take me out on a date that Saturday evening. Naturally, I obliged and began my week-long special occasion preparation ritual: my legs were shaved, I was waxed like a mannequin, and I got a new outfit. The fated day came and . . . *crickets.*

If someone asks you out on a date without any sincere enthusiasm and offers no details regarding time and location, *you aren't going out on a date.* Don't shave your legs or your armpits. Do not waste your makeup. Thank you for coming to my TED talk.

*The Boy from Bumble* ghosted me after two weeks of incredible conversations and witty banter. He freakin' *ghosted* me. What was the main takeaway about ghosting I advised previously? You can't let it get you down (forever) even though it totally feels like—and is—a slap in the face.

Thanks to my commitment to loving myself, knowing my worth, and fully believing the Universe had my back and had an amazing man on the way, I didn't let this get me down. I know it may sound crazy, but I honestly *knew* the guy of my dreams existed for me and that I deserved him. Obviously, this guy who ghosted me wasn't that person. So, I sent him a polite message letting him know that I wasn't interested in someone who played those types of games and wished him all the best a la the option A advice I gave in chapter 17. Ding! Ding! Ding! Oh, did he *try* to win me back. After a week of him apologizing profusely and begging to make it up to me, I reluctantly agreed to an hour with him. It was a Monday night, I didn't shave my legs, I barely wore any makeup, and I wore workout clothes to our date. Seriously, we're talking minimal effort here, although I did wear tight leggings and a crop top, so it wasn't like I was a frumpy mess waiting for him in the parking lot.

He got out of his car to wave at me, and I was stunned—*to say the least.* The ghost from Bumble smiling back at me was *way* hotter than any of the pictures on his profile. Seriously, he was the anti-catfish. I could not form words. I literally did not speak for the first two minutes of our date. Really it was a class-act showing from me: dressed in workout clothes and completely mute. Just what every super-hot guy who's interested in something serious wants, right? Luckily, I was able to get my shit together and finally speak in sentences, and we went on to have the greatest last first date of all time. (Yes, *my husband ghosted me*—again, the Universe: big sense of humor. And trust me, I don't ever let him forget this fact—it works wonders for my shoe closet.)

By the end of the date, I was a seriously smitten kitten. As we were bidding each other goodbye, we made plans to see each other the next day. I asked him where he lived and when he named the same apartment complex I had been living in for eight months, I almost choked on my own spit. We were living feet away from each other for eight months! We had texted each other while lying by the *same* pool, knowing the other person was at a pool. Who knows how many times we just missed each other at the mailboxes or the fitness center? I'm willing to bet the Universe was getting a little, ahem, frustrated by our lack of awareness and took control of the matter, per usual.

Beyond the jarring realization we lived in the same complex, we also discovered we had moved in on the same day (weird) and had the same area rug in our apartments (weirder). On a scale of one to really fucking aligned, we were beyond the scale. The Universe was not messing around and gave me no opportunity to think, "Well, I don't know about him." I asked the Universe for what I wanted, and it definitely delivered.

The first step to getting what (or who) you want is to know what the hell that is. **You can't ask for something if you don't know what you're asking for.** It would be like walking into a Starbucks and being like, "Well, I don't know . . . whatever you think would be good for me." The poor barista does not get paid enough to deal with those kinds of antics. The Universe (while it *does* know what's best for you) is waiting for you to *ask* for it. What do you want? I mean, truly—deep down—what would set your soul on fire? Is it an emotionally available man with a steady job, income, and an incredibly beautiful dick? Is it a patient person who has no interest in marriage but is seeking a funny date for a long-term relationship? Is it a girlboss CEO who definitely wants to get married but doesn't want kids? Is it a fellow divorced person who understands the complexity of divorce but hasn't given up on finding their life partner? What do you want? The Universe is on stage at a Spice Girls concert singing, "So tell me what you want . . . what you really, really want!" waiting for you to, you know, respond. Figure out whatever (or whoever) it is you want and *ask*. This isn't about what your parents want, what your friends think, or what your co-workers advise: this is about *you* and what you not only want, but deserve.

Feeling worthy of whatever it is you want is one of the most important parts of manifesting your dreams. Often, we've been burned by so many losers and ghosted by so many jerks that we can lose sight of what we actually deserve. We get used to the games and antics and it can feel like there's no end in sight—that this is, you know, *it*. Well, it isn't it. Stop settling and stop sabotaging. **You deserve the fucking world.** You deserve a French billionaire who gives you three orgasms. You deserve to be a billionaire yourself!

You deserve an emotionally available, gorgeous unicorn of an individual who worships the ground you walk on. You deserve someone who looks at you the way a basic betch looks at sizzling truffle fries arriving at her table. You deserve it all. Do you fully *believe* you are worthy of something so amazing? If you don't, figure out how you can get there. Repeat affirmations to yourself daily, every minute, or whatever it takes to change your mindset from "Oh, I don't know" to "I deserve the freakin' world, and I'm amazing because I'm me!" You are *you. That* is your superpower.

Once you fully step into the idea that you are worthy of your dream, you have to wholeheartedly believe that there's no way it won't happen for you. It's simply impossible for it to be impossible. Your belief in its reality must be so unwavering that any bump or pothole in the road doesn't deter you. Even if all the evidence points to something being out of reach, it doesn't matter because you know it isn't. Having faith in the unseen is easier said than done, especially if our line of sight (or rearview mirror) is full of bad experiences. Look beyond those unhappy moments, think bigger, and believe the partner and the epic life of your dreams exists for you—because it can. Tell the Universe exactly what you want and believe it will bring it to your front door because you deserve it.

The Law of Attraction only works when you believe in the certainty of something that is often totally uncertain. Your mind is the key to attracting epic love, but it also can keep you right where you are. It's honestly up to you to make your life the best it can be. Think about this: do you want to be ninety-two and regret not dreaming big and going after it? Picture yourself five years from now as someone who didn't ask for what they really wanted and never believed it was possible. You're working the same job, dating the same kinds of people, and living in the same place. How does it feel? Alternatively, visualize yourself five years from now as the person who asked for what they wanted, believed it was already theirs, and fully committed to it. Picture yourself being hugely successful, in an epic relationship, rich, and all of the things. How does that feel versus the former? (I'm guessing, ahem, much better!)

I *know* it's hard and seems impossible. I, too, once thought manifesting something was impossible until I realized I had, you know, manifested the man of my dreams. I became laser focused on what I wanted and finally stepped into believing that it would come true for me. The only other option was to live the life I'd already been living, and I didn't like the idea of that. The Universe has a person for you: ask for that person, and then sit back, relax, and pop some bubbly. You might have to endure a few mediocre dates in the meantime, but when the Universe gives you what you asked for, you're not going to have any questions or concerns.

**If you find yourself feeling unsure or confused—you have your answer.** It probably isn't it. Clarity comes naturally when something works. The Universe isn't playing around with your forever person. It will be a full-body *yes*. Can you imagine if I asked the Universe for a sign that my (now) husband was the one? It would be all, "Huh? You mean, beyond the *instant* connection, the same apartment complex, same rug, and same move-in date weren't enough for you?" It would have been ridiculous for me not to be 100% all in. Was it scary? Of course it was. Matters of the heart are scary, especially when it's with someone who, you know, is really fucking awesome. You deserve someone *that* awesome, and that awesome person *is* out there looking for someone exactly like you. The Universe knows it, I know it, but do *you* know it? It's beyond time to start believing and begin manifesting the epic love (and life) of your dreams.

# Chapter 23—
# Your Mind Should Be like the Perfect Mimosa: Clear as Fuck

*You must first see a thing clearly in your mind before you can do it.*
*—Alex Morrison*

If you're single and have been for any amount of time, you're likely familiar with some V. annoying comments (usually by people who have been married for seventeen years and have no idea what ghosting even means): "It'll happen when you least expect it" and, my personal least favorite, "when you know, *you know.*" I got to the point where I imagined myself punching someone in the face if they said anything like that to me. Unfortunately, I'm now one of those married people who drank the love Kool-Aid because, well, it *did* happen when I least expected it, and I most definitely *knew.* It's okay if you want to punch me in the face.

I was so sure that my now-husband was the one that I sent *my mother* a text message post first date claiming, "I just met the man I'm gonna marry." Cue the eye roll and vomiting, but feel free to reach out to her; she'll confirm this is not an exaggeration. Normally, I wouldn't dare tell my mom about a first date, seventh date, or whatever date until I was sure he wasn't, you know, going anywhere. I had decided that I wasn't getting my parents involved in my love life anymore after my failure with their almost-son-in-law Smooth and my long bout of back-to-back-to-back fuckboys. You might know the feeling yourself when Harry from Hinge or Bonnie from Bumble—who both ghosted you after two dates—get brought up at dinner or during a phone call. There comes a point in your life when it's no longer worth talking about it. Plus, quite frankly, anyone who isn't familiar with how much dating has changed couldn't possibly relate.

Why on earth would I reach out to my mom with such a bold statement moments after our first encounter? Because The Boy from Bumble was a living, breathing, *real-life* version of my perfect man mental vision board. It was as if he had been assembled at Mikaela's Future Husband Factory and came out as this bearded, naturally tanned, and perfectly chiseled Captain America look-a-like. Beyond looks, his personality was both exactly what I was looking for and exactly what I *needed*—down to the very last detail. Every single thing I had written down, imagined, and *felt* would make the ideal partner was staring right back at me, filling my wine glass, and offering me a piece of cured meat (my love for charcuterie runs very deep and started way back when I would beg my mother to buy me Lunchables and SunnyD at Albertsons on the grocery run). Every single detail I had listed to the Universe was somehow seamlessly woven together into the man of my dreams, and he was the furthest thing from the fuckboys I was so used to. When you meet the right person, it might feel like it's way too good to be true, even though it is V. real.

I knew in my soul that The Boy from Bumble was the one because there wasn't a single missing detail. Of course, he has his flaws—as do I and the rest of the population. This is beside the point. The thing is: **the Universe *loves* details.** The Universe doesn't do well with vague requests because, well, if there's any room for interpretation, the Universe is most likely going to take it. Let's say your only request to the Universe is: please, please just *not* a fuckboy—I want an emotionally available man who is ready for something serious! The Universe responds willingly, "Okay, easy peasy, lemon squeezy!" and sends you someone emotionally available but you're not physically attracted to them. Let's be honest, physical attraction is a crucial part of a relationship. While looks aren't everything, don't you want to be hot for someone who might have the last naked body you see in your life? Don't you want to get butterflies around someone even after twenty years have gone by? Sure, looks will fade and we all get older, but physical attraction helps keep the spice alive in a relationship.

How great would it be to be that old couple who still act like they get it on regularly? Maybe he slaps her butt when they get up from dinner or she gives him googly eyes when he's on the treadmill. I'd prefer to be part of *that* twosome instead of the pair who only have sex on special occasions. As we learned in chapter 4, spectacular sex is something all of us deserve.

When you're experimenting with the possibilities of the Law of Attraction and decide you're going to manifest something, be specific. I mean, be *very specific*. List every single detail you can think of, whether it's your dream partner, dream job, dream house, whatever. Make a freakin' vision board and visualize! What are in the nooks and crannies of this desire of yours? Write it down. Cut pictures from magazines or copy and paste photos you find online.

If it elicits an emotional reaction (of the good variety), even better. Take it all in. You need to get crystal fucking clear about what you want. What does it look like, sound like, taste like, and *feel* like? You get the picture. Use every single one of your senses to tap into whatever it is. Think of it like your own personal Pinterest board all about your desires, your dreams, your future—your epic life.

How clear do you need to get? You need to get as clear as a correctly prepared mimosa. Like most millennials, brunch is my favorite food group, and the best kind of brunch involves champagne, normally in the form of a mimosa. We don't do rookie mimosas here, right? We don't mix half orange juice and half champagne or use even a one-to-three ratio. The perfect mimosa is 99% champagne and 1% orange juice. It's basically champagne, with a hint of vitamin C (for health purposes). A correctly prepared mimosa is clear as fuck. Just like a mimosa, your mind has to be *so* clear about what you want, that you're basically sending it on a silver platter to the Universe, who answers, "Oh, okay, comin' right up!" and gets to work making that very thing a very real reality.

While it's V. important to think about all the things you want, it's even more valuable to consider what it is you *need*. For me, I needed a man who was calm, reliable, and secure. Because of my past, I can still be triggered by things sometimes. Healing isn't linear and, despite the work I've done, there are days when I'm not firing on all cylinders and the anxiety is really heavy. Having a steady, stable partner is something that helps me feel safe in the moments I'm having an emotional response. I don't worry about my husband leaving me or feel overwhelmed when this happens. His prevailing calming, level-headed energy helps me relax. Can you imagine if I didn't consider this when thinking of my ideal partner? If I ended up with someone who was emotional or highly reactive, it would likely make matters worse. For example, if I was acting out, he'd probably respond with heightened emotions, which would stress me out even more and probably make me want to retreat and shut down.

In the same way his calming energy is helpful to me during emotional situations, my ability to communicate emotions helps him. As an emotional person, I encourage him to come out of his shell and communicate his feelings more. He's the rational to my emotional, and I'm the exact opposite to him. We bring out the best in each other instead of highlighting the worst.

For years, I had been looking for someone to complete me—someone who could correct parts of me I considered "wrong" or "bad." While we all have aspects of ourselves that may need a little improvement, those aspects don't make us bad, and they certainly don't mean we require another person to come in and fix us like we are a leaky kitchen sink. First and foremost, the only person who is capable of changing something about you is you. It is equally important to understand that you are complete all by yourself. You don't need anyone else to make you whole. That said, you *can* want to attract someone who not only loves you for who you are (as we examined in chapter 5), but also enhances your amazing qualities *and* supports you while you work through the things you want to change. What kind of person could do this for you? What are their characteristics?

Considering what you need isn't always an easy process, especially if you have to address something you're not exactly proud of.

That said, being crystal clear can only happen if you're 100% honest with yourself. If you're someone who hates to cook and clean (and you aren't planning on becoming the next Martha Stewart overnight), you are not going to be a good fit for someone who is working all the time and would love some help with the household chores. This person is going to feel love through acts of service that make their day a little easier—things like doing their laundry, preparing their meals, and making sure they have a clean house to come home to. I know it's not 1952, but the reality remains this is what some people are looking for. Maybe you want to be the breadwinner bringing home all of the bacon because you're career-driven and successful. You might need someone who is okay with not being the breadwinner of the household and instead has dinner and a heavy glass of wine ready for you every night when you come home from work. Or perhaps you both can be badasses at work, and you hire a chef or someone to clean your house regularly. Whatever it is, it doesn't matter as long as you are addressing what you both need.

Getting clear in the details is essential when manifesting something because if you leave something open to interpretation, the Universe will typically take it and run with it. You won't have the iconic when-you-know-you-know moment. It'll be more like, "Well, I mean, I guess this is probably it." It sounds confusing because it is. You won't be sure if this is it or not. Maybe you'll find yourself asking the Universe for a sign that this is, you know, *it*. I'd prefer the other side of the coin where it's a full-blown, resounding *yes* from my higher self, not needing any signs from the Universe because it gave me exactly what I wanted. Bear in mind, the Universe knows best. Maybe it sent you what you didn't realize you needed. Even though this person isn't exactly what you had initially pictured, your body and mind are both sending you a resounding yes. You've started to pay attention to your intuition, and your higher self is so proud of you for finally making the right choice instead of leveling down with the good-for-nothing losers of your relationship past.

The process of believing that whatever you want can happen for you starts with telling the Universe what you want and knowing deep down that you are totally and unequivocally deserving of whatever it is. Now you see the importance of being V. clear about what you desire when you're asking for it. You've engaged all your senses here and tapped into how it's going to feel when you get it. When you tap into that feeling, the moment you get it is going to feel oddly familiar because it has already happened in your mind. If it doesn't exist in your mind, it can't exist in your line of sight. Twilight zone? Absolutely. Speaking of *Twilight*, while you might not be into the whole Bella and Edward love story, you've got to admit that they were drawn to each other in a totally cosmic way. That's exactly how it feels when you've gotten uber clear about what you want. So, when it shows up, there isn't any confusion or lack of clarity. You are seeing a physical form of what you already created in your mind.

The Law of Attraction works because our brains have the power to create a reality wilder than our wildest dreams. Many, if not most of us, know Jim Carrey as an uber successful actor and innately funny human being. While he is both of these things, he's also someone who is a living, breathing example of the extreme power of the Law of Attraction and exactly how much the Universe responds to details. Mr. Carrey wasn't always successful; in fact, there was a time when he was struggling financially and flopping all of his comedy gigs. Our pal Jim didn't let that reality get him down, even though no one would have blamed him if he did. Instead, he wrote himself a check for ten million dollars (!!!) and dated it ten years in the future (!!!) for "acting services rendered." He signed the check, put it in his wallet, and went about his life. Wouldn't you know it, in November 1995 (ahem, ten years later), Jim Carrey was cast in the iconic movie *Dumb and Dumber* and received a check for—drum roll, please—ten million dollars. Talk about the Universe responding to details!

Humans have a consciousness for a reason and, unfortunately, it's under-utilized by most people. **Your mind is your most valuable weapon.** Write yourself a check for ten million dollars, make yourself a vision board, detail your dream life in the Notes app on your iPhone, practice the speech you're going to give at Harvard for the class of 2025, or whatever. We have the power to create a reality that makes us want to close our eyes and bury our heads in the sand *or* a reality that makes us jump out of bed in the morning because we're so freakin' excited that this is our life. If you have the power to create both realities, wouldn't you want to choose the latter?

The time is now to get V. clear about whatever it is that you desire. You can think of everything. It should be so crazy and outlandish that you have no idea how the hell it's possible for something (or someone) so great to exist. You should be giddy thinking about it and so pumped up at the idea that it exists *for you.* Pop open some Veuve and get to thinking. Go ahead and think big! The Universe favors the bold, so you might as well go all out.

# Chapter 24—
# The Universe Has a Unique Sense of Humor

*You may have to fight a battle more than once to win it.*
*—Margaret Thatcher*

When I first hopped onto the I'm-going-to-manifest-anything-I-want bandwagon, I was quickly met with the unpleasant reality that, well, it's not going to be as easy as 1-2-3 and poof! There's my husband dusting the sparkles off his button-down shirt. Though it would be amazing to wake up with a brand-new Audi Q5 in the garage and Chris Evans or Idris Elba (or dare I say, *both*) waiting for me in bed, the Universe doesn't exactly work like that. Sometimes, it can be more simple than it is a challenge: we ask for something and we receive it quicker than we might have expected. Poof! An Idris Elba look-a-like strolls into the bookstore and reaches for the very book you have been trying to find for fifteen minutes. Other times, particularly when it's a really big dream, goal, or desire, the Universe, ahem, likes to see how committed we are to the belief that it's already ours and on the way. As I've mentioned, the Universe has a V. unique sense of humor that can be hard to understand in the moment we're front and center at its sold-out comedy show. It can make us confused and frustrated, and we wonder if said "humor" is actually a sign from the Universe that we're not on the right path. The Universe, however, is giggling away knowing that what we want is just behind this roadblock, this pothole, or this really fucking huge storm we're currently dealing with.

When you've gone through the process of healing, forgiving, and being fully committed to this new journey you're on, the Universe is likely going to throw some hurdles your way to test how committed you are to getting what you desire and to ensure you are ready for it. These hurdles will look V. different for everyone, but the reason they appear is to make sure your belief that whatever you want is on its way to you is as unwavering as a basic betch's love for brunch on the weekends. Basically, you have to be strong AF, despite whatever comes your way. Things might be going up in flames, but do not take this as a sign from the Universe that you won't ever get what you want or that you're not on the right track. Do you remember when I told you that your mindset is something you have to work on ev-er-y-day, kind of like doing squats all the time for a juicy booty? I wrote that for a reason: manifesting your dreams (especially the really big ones like an epic love) is going to be a lot more grueling if you haven't been working on your mental squats on the regular. Luckily, you, my darling, are strong and you can do mental squats like nobody's business.

To give you an idea of just how weird the Universe's sense of humor can get, I'll run through a few of the hurdles I faced on my own personal journey to epic love. First and foremost, the number of fuckboys I swiped right on and went out on dates with was astounding. Fuckboys, as we know, are everywhere and I'm quite certain I met every single one who resides in Las Vegas (which might actually be the capital of Fuckboy-ville, USA). I had gotten so clear about what I wanted, had constantly recalibrated my vibration, and was totally happy and grateful. I felt all the feels of what it would be like to be in the perfect relationship with the man of my dreams. The number of daily affirmations I repeated to myself would have overwhelmed most people. So when all of these seemingly great guys ended up being the same kind of guy I was trying to avoid, I worried I was doing something wrong, or worse, that maybe this was just the Universe's way of setting me straight.

Nope! No freakin' way. I refused to believe that story. While it certainly would have been serendipitous to meet my now husband *the day we moved into the same apartment complex*, the Universe had another plan in mind. It's not our responsibility to understand why or how. We just need to believe that:

a) the Universe is always on our side,
and
b) we deserve everything we desire, and it's already on the way.

The Universe can and will handle the rest. It also enjoys sending some lessons our way. In my case, that lesson came in the form of a fuckboy who appeared to be a totally eligible, emotionally available man.

I had been seeing *The Chameleon* for a little over a month, and things were going great. While I wasn't immediately physically attracted to him, I was V. much drawn to his personality, charm, and intelligence. We had a lot in common (or so I thought), and after a few dates, my physical attraction grew. Sparks began to fly. He showed me places in Las Vegas I had never been, he frequently showered me with gifts, and we could talk for hours on end without feeling overwhelmed or bored. He was intent on making things official, but I was still getting used to my newfound confidence and the idea of self-love and decided I needed a little more time. (In retrospect, this was my intuition signaling that I needed to move on despite the lack of obvious red flags.)

One night, I had a frightening, life-threatening encounter with the toxic ex-boyfriend I briefly mentioned in chapter 20. I was scared—to put it lightly. I told The Chameleon what had happened and that I needed some space so I could process the incident on my own (and with my therapist). He didn't react like the supportive and kind man I thought him to be. Instead, he was judgmental and unkind, and he made me feel like this situation was my fault. He got angry because I asked for space and insinuated that he was never really that into me, that I needed help, and he was happy he had continued to date other women during our brief romance. I don't know whether his response was a result of his ego feeling a little bruised from my request or if he really felt that way, but his true colors were exposed during that conversation. We didn't see each other again. In the following days, I silently wished him well in the future (and hoped he would learn some social etiquette during uncomfortable conversations). I forgave him; I also forgave myself for ignoring my own intuition and thanked the Universe for the lesson. Maybe it was just making sure my relationship picker had been set straight.

Another questionable experience on my journey was being hit by a car one morning on my way to work. While I'm happy to report

I made it out relatively okay, at the time I was all, "WHAT THE HECK IS THIS ABOUT, UNIVERSE?" Any sane person would have thought, "Okay, let's change gears, pivot, and try something different because this clearly isn't doing the trick." Swiping right on fuckboys is one thing, but a car accident? Despite our newly acquired understanding of the limitlessness of the Universe, the not-so-great parts of life are inevitable. Instead of it totally ruining your new abundant mindset, maybe you can think, "Oh, you think I can't handle this, Universe? WATCH ME!" Then laugh all the way to the bank when the insurance check comes in, because the person who hit you ran a red light and that's, you know, illegal. All the signs might be pointing to exit, stage left, but it's really just the Universe checking in and making sure you're steady in your belief. It's easy to believe in something when things are dandy and easy and sparkling in the sunlight like a suncatcher during golden hour. It's not so easy to believe when you're calling a tow truck, fuckboys are flooding your DMs, and you have no idea how the hell you're going to get to work on time. That's why you need faith—you need to believe in the unseen. You're not always going to see what you want right away, even though you are doing all the right things.

One of the worst things I experienced on my journey was the loss of an old friendship. It almost made me give up. The Universe had sent fuckboys and an errant driver—fine—but a bitter end to a friendship of fifteen years? It just seemed like too much. Losing a friendship is like a breakup, because, well, *you break up*. What I came to realize later is that this was the Universe's unique way of ensuring I had really learned how to face my emotions, feel them, let them go, and—most importantly—I had learned to forgive. I had to do all those things for the people who had hurt me in my love life, but for whatever reason, this situation stung the most. It stung because there wasn't a reason beyond the fact that we just weren't on the same path any longer and neither of us wanted to change course to join the other. Semi-begrudgingly, I faced the emotions instead of what I wanted to do (avoid them). I wished her all the best and forgave her for the pain she caused me. Wouldn't you know it, I felt lighter after that. Forgiveness really is freedom.

I learned a very valuable lesson from this: when someone or something is removed from your life, space is made for someone or something else to enter your life. While I understand this idea won't necessarily make the departure enjoyable (by any stretch of the imagination), I hope it will provide you some solace when dealing with the discomfort. If you're feeling sad about a loss, remind yourself that the Universe just needed some room for what you've been asking for.

This isn't a one-time sort of thing, either. My biggest dream of becoming a successful author was honestly a little more challenging than manifesting the man of my dreams. I faced a year filled with rejection, judgment, embarrassment, shame, and a whole lot of storms making me question if the Universe was trying to nudge me in another direction. I spent so many days and nights crying and wondering if I should give up. At one point, I accidentally deleted an *entire* chapter of edits—a day of work that I couldn't recover—and had to start over from scratch. I won't lie, there were initially some cuss words flying around, but I decided to take a chapter out of my own book (pun intended) and trust that the Universe was making sure I wasn't going to give up on my dream because of a dumb user error. The point is, despite a whole fuck ton of evidence suggesting I should give up and throw in the I'm-gonna-be-an-author towel, I didn't. Considering you're reading this very paragraph, it seems like the Universe was just *really* trying to test my commitment and belief that this grand dream of mine could become a reality.

The storms you face on your journey will be different from the ones I experienced. We're all on our own paths here. But you *will* face them, whether they're Category 5 hurricanes or quick tropical cloudbursts that keep things perfectly green in the Caribbean. While no storm—big or small—is exactly pleasant to stand in (especially with no umbrella in sight), one thing remains true: the air is always cleaner once it passes, and for some, there's a beautiful rainbow.

The metaphorical cleaner air following a storm could also be a redirection that helps you discover something new—a different trajectory that takes you down a path that has what's meant for you at the end. You could come up with a totally new idea that flows like a waterfall into your brain. For example, maybe you thought epic love meant security and empowerment, but it really means something totally different to you. Alternatively, you might have an epiphany and discover the thing you've been looking for was right in front of your face all along. It's the calm after the storm—you can see things so much more clearly at that point.

For example, one of my best friends found herself in a seven-year relationship turned engagement that, ahem, none of her friends or family were too excited about. While there were a lot of negative things that had transpired throughout their time together, it boiled down to the fact that he, frankly, was not her forever person, despite having spent so much time together and the fact that a wedding was on the way. She went through a pretty awful storm that ended with a broken engagement just weeks before her planned wedding day. Um, not exactly ideal, especially if you know how much a wedding costs these days. As a former wedding planner, I can tell you it's V. expensive (much more expensive than you think). Following this, she was understandably upset, but the clarity she experienced as a result was pretty fascinating to watch from the outside. She didn't hop right into dating, but when she finally did, she ended up meeting her hubby on Bumble and got married eight months later. She never would have met her true forever person if she hadn't faced the storm the Universe sent her to bring the clarity she needed to see what her family and friends already saw so clearly. I'm happy to report she's still (very) happily married, and I wouldn't be surprised if I got a FaceTime announcing a positive pregnancy test soon. (Fun fact: I sent this paragraph to my BFF so she could review it and give me permission to include it in the book. She had been resigned to the fact that they would have to try IVF but on the *exact* day that I sent it to her, she found out that she was pregnant! The. Frickin'. Universe.)

The magic happens when there's a rainbow after you face your storm. The rainbow is exactly what you think it is: your dream becoming a reality. No longer is it something that was only in your head—now he's standing in front of you, six foot two inches of pure sex appeal . . . oh, sorry, that was just the pot of gold at the end of *my* rainbow. All jokes aside, rainbows happen every day, and multiple times a day at that. But they can't exist without some rain—even

Dolly Parton knew that when she said, "The way I see it, if you want the rainbow, you gotta put up with the rain." So she must be a spiritual junkie, too. The reason the saying "A smooth sea never made for a skilled sailor" has stayed with us for as long as it has is because no one ever gets good at something without having to work at it, especially when it's really fucking hard.

When things don't seem to be going your way, and you feel like you might lose it if you find yourself across the table from *yet* another terrible date, remind yourself that you are a skilled sailor, and if anyone can get through this, it's you. Ugh, I know. You aren't here for a motivational pep talk, but the truth is that you are *far* stronger than you think. Hell, I know all the fuckboys I had to deal with made me a strong-ass woman. Believing in the possible when it seems impossible is your way of telling the Universe you're *more* than ready to feel the calm after the storm or accept the rainbow about to come your way. The Universe's sense of humor is not for the faint of heart, but you have all the tools you need to stay strong. Whether it's cleaner air or a beautiful double rainbow, the other side of any storm is so worth the bad weather.

# Chapter 25—
# Now That You Know What You Want, You Kinda-Sorta-Totally Have to Forget About It

*Surrender is a gift that you can give yourself. It's an act of faith. It's saying that even though I can't see where this river is flowing, I trust it will take me in the right direction.*
*—Debbie Ford*

Sometimes the most important things to do are also the most difficult things to do. The hardest part about manifesting anything, especially big, life-changing things, is that once you've gotten clear about what you want and have asked the Universe to send it your way—and you believe it's going to happen despite everything suggesting otherwise—you have to completely detach from the how and the when of getting whatever it is you want. Yes, you read that correctly: you have to focus on the vision of your dream intently and then basically let go and carry on with your life trusting that the Universe has your back. I, too, wish I was kidding; but, unfortunately, it's totally the case.

I've been a control freak for, well, my entire life. I envy anyone who is Type B (for example, my husband) who can la-dee-dah through life, go with the flow, and make everything look like it's a piece of cake. Me, on the other hand, I have everything planned down to the second, am always arriving five to fifteen minutes early, and have a panic attack when things don't go exactly as planned. We all have *that* friend, right? If you were wondering how I felt about the whole if-you-want-to-manifest-something-you-have-to-let-it-go-and-surrender-to-the-Universe thing, I was *not* enthused!

I had already done the hard stuff: faced the past head on and felt all the emotions and processed them. I had acknowledged some habits that, you know, weren't all that great and committed to changing them. I even fully forgave all the men from my checkered past and forgave myself for all the mistakes I had made. I got my mind right. I was a reformed serial fuckboy dater, semi-reformed perfectionist, and kinda-sort-of-but-not-really reformed control freak. I knew exactly what I wanted and needed. I believed I deserved it and that the Universe would bring it to me. I had done it all—except, well, the most important thing.

It was all I thought about, all the time. I'd anxiously walk into Starbucks, ready for Mr. Forever to bump into me on the way out. I'd settle into happy hour waiting for him to buy me a drink. I'd walk through the crowded Las Vegas strip, eyes darting left and right, waiting for the Universe to send him. I was ready! What I didn't realize at the time was that I was trying to drive a bus that I didn't know how to drive—I didn't even have the damn keys to turn on the engine. I was trying to direct the show and control the outcome—and I was blocking the Universe from stepping in and taking care of it for me. I asked the Universe for a cup of sugar and, when it came to the door with a five-pound bag, I shut the door in its face. I was frustrated and without sugar, which, you know, isn't a great place to be when you're thirty and undeniably single.

Sometimes if you focus too hard on how or when something is going to happen, you can get caught up trying to control something that you simply cannot ever control. It would be like me swimming out into the ocean thinking I could control a sixty-foot wave in front of me by making it stop and go in the other direction. I'm physically, mentally, and emotionally incapable of making a sixty-foot wave go in the opposite direction because it's a sixty-foot wave and I'm only slightly over sixty inches (even if I'm sixty inches of badass female). The Universe is *way* bigger than a sixty-foot wave, mmkay?

I had to *surrender.* I had to let go and let the Universe take over. Surrendering control is awfully hard to do when

a) you're a control freak,

and

b) you *really* want something to happen.

Here's the thing: the Universe knows the whole damn story. It doesn't have to connect the dots because it sees the entire painting—and the whole museum for that matter. The Universe knows way better than you or I could ever *dream*. For me, surrendering wasn't as simple as, "Okay, I'm just going to stop thinking about it!" because, well, that just wouldn't have worked out. When someone tells you *not* to look at something, you immediately want to look at that thing. What can I say—we're only human. Knowing myself and how letting go of control was going to be V. hard for me, I decided to put my focus into something else while continuing to believe I would get what I wanted—something that would take my mind off manifesting the perfect person for me. It needed to be something so consuming that my mind would naturally focus on it instead of wondering when the hell the Universe was going to come through for me. So, I began to write.

The first eight chapters of this book were written before I met my husband (along with a couple of other chapters that didn't end up making the cut but did offer me a lot of lessons I needed to learn). I had written a little over twenty thousand words before I hopped on Bumble and swiped right on the man of my dreams. I had spent months writing, and it became all that I could think about. I was reflecting on the past but enjoying the present. I wrote when I got home from work. I wrote on the weekend. I was constantly typing ideas into my iPhone Notes app when something stirred in me—whether I was on a walk, watching a movie, or just passing the time at work.

It was at the very moment I took my focus off how or when I would find the perfect guy that I met him. The Universe had been working behind the scenes for a while, but I needed to learn the ultimate lesson before it sent him my way. I needed to learn the importance of *surrender*: the crucial art of letting go; the act of freeing yourself from the outcome you want—and being okay with the idea you might never get it. I became so focused on the idea of writing a book and becoming an author one day that I honestly did not think *once* about being single forever. I just believed my person was out there, somewhere. A few months earlier, finding my soulmate seemed like the *only* thing I could think about; but when I began writing my energy lit up like a Christmas tree, and the Universe loves to see that level of vibration.

If you fully desire something, it's destined for you. I know there are a million books out there full of tips and tricks about how to get the guy or the girl. I know this because I read them all and, well, still found myself without the guy. This goes beyond new flirting tactics and how to reel the person in. This is about *attracting* your person into your reality. Like attracts like, so you'll want your vibration to match the person you are looking for—this is why it's crucial to monitor your frequency and adjust it when necessary. For the Law of Attraction to work, you must let go. You must detach from the how, the when, and even the exact outcome you have in mind. In my case, that meant accepting the fact that I might never meet *the guy,* and I might be single forever. Not exactly the easiest thing for a hopeless romantic whose most frequented TV channel is the Hallmark channel, particularly around the holidays.

When you surrender to the Universe, you acknowledge that it knows best, and you *believe* in it 100%. You're like, "Yes, Universe, I know you have my back on this one!" and go on your merry way, kissing babies, waving at all your fans, skipping along, and smelling the roses.

Hard? Extremely.

Important? Entirely.

If you're having a difficult time surrendering because it's, well, really fucking difficult, you can acknowledge your struggle. It always comes back to awareness. In order to detach from the outcome, you have to recognize how it is you are attached. Be brutally honest with yourself: are you obsessing over the when and how? Are you focusing on the outcome as if your life depends on it? Are you trying to maintain total control? Focus on how that makes you feel. For me, I was in a constant state of anxiety thinking about everything I wanted and wondering when the heck it would be mine. Anxiety, my darling, is *not* vibrating at a high frequency.

Anxiety and other low-level emotions aren't serving you and might be blocking you from manifesting *all* of the things. Once you acknowledge this, you can gently tell the Universe you're surrendering your attachment. Repeat it multiple times a day. Hell, repeat it all the freakin' time if you have to. Say it out loud. Repeat it whenever you catch yourself trying to control something or are totally hung up on the outcome. In my experience, the more important something is to me, the more I need to remind myself that the Universe is working on getting it for me and I have to *let go.* I have got to surrender. This crazy simple thing will immediately shift your energy. When I do this, it's almost like a weight has been lifted off my shoulders because I no longer have all the responsibility. I trust that the Universe will only send me something that will benefit me. I'm vibrating at the same level as the Universe and allowing it to work its magic. I don't know about you, but I *love* magic.

Something important to keep in mind here: the Universe is either going to:

a) bring you exactly what you asked for,

or

b) bring you something *even better.*

Um . . . how fucking awesome is that?

To help me detach from the outcome, I brought something into my life that changed my focus from finding a husband to finding my passion. I realized that when I was writing, I immediately started to light up. My energy was through the freakin' roof! The Universe was probably like, "It's about damn time you found your calling. Next up: the man of your dreams!" While I was busy doing something that made me feel happy and like I had a purpose, the Universe was busy, you know, manifesting my dream. I was also busy being exactly the kind of woman my future hubby was looking for. (Ahem, vibration!) I just had no idea I was doing it. All I knew was that I loved what I was doing, and it felt damn good not to be so worried about love anymore. I was so proud of how far I had come; writing allowed me to really see that in full.

**The miracles in life happen when we least expect it.** I know it's hard to let go, but imagine the possibilities for when you do: you'll either get whatever it is you've asked for or something even better. Surrender to the Universe and detach from the outcome you desire. Seriously, let it go. You are Elsa, spinning around, icicles dancing around you. Find something else to focus on. We live in a world that has a lot of options. What's something you always wanted to do but could never find the time for? Or, what's something you loved as a kid but stopped doing for one reason or another? What's something that you get so engrossed in that time seems to stand still while you're doing it? Do that thing! Do it because it makes you happy and it lights you up. Do it because you deserve to feel happy and free. The Universe is going to notice—and, well, you might be surprised at what happens when you're not looking.

# Chapter 26—
# Gratitude: For the Person You Have Become and For the Gifts the Universe Brings You

*It's a funny thing about life, once you begin to take note of things you are grateful for, you begin to lose sight of the things that you lack.*
*—Germany Kent*

The funny thing about a transformative journey is you never quite realize you're on one until you've found yourself at the end, or at least at a new beginning. I began my journey on my kitchen floor, only because I knew I didn't want to ever feel like that again. If you had told *that girl* she'd not only soon meet the epic love of her life, but also finally let go of the pain she had felt for years, she would have scoffed at the idea because it wouldn't have felt remotely possible. That's the thing we need to remind ourselves of all the time: even the most impossible of ideas are *totally* possible. That said, the Universe will make damn sure you've learned all the lessons before, you know, you get to the other side. For me, the Universe tested me in the form of a vacation in Napa. I, too, realize how ridiculous that sounds; I recognize a vacation in Napa is a privilege—just like my vacation with my parents in the Caribbean was. I was so lucky to experience both of these things, but each experience provided a lesson that I think is worth sharing with you.

Early on, soon after I met my now husband, my then (very hunky) boyfriend and I were lounging by the pool talking about nothing too important when I looked at the bottle of wine we were drinking. It was a Napa Valley wine. I remember I sighed and remarked, "God I'd love to go to Napa someday," and thought about the green vines, the warm sunshine, and took a sip of the chilled wine. It tasted fabulous, as it always does, and I pictured myself running through the vineyards like some sort of basic betch because, if you haven't noticed by now, I am a basic betch. And then I went on chatting about whatever the hell we were talking about because, you know, wine buzz is a total thing. I didn't think anything of it, except I felt grateful for the fact that I *knew* one day I would finally go to Napa and enjoy the hell out of it.

Well, the Universe heard me loud and clear because I found myself in Northern California wine country a few months later. I said what I wanted, envisioned it in my mind, knew that I'd make it there one day, and then I totally forgot I had even mentioned it. My incredibly considerate other half didn't forget because he secretly planned the whole thing (cue the Hallmark-worthy swoons). As we now have come to realize, not being in control, particularly on a vacation, is very difficult for me. But, when you're going to Napa, sometimes you just gotta . . . let go (and let the Universe drive). I told myself that no matter what happened, I would be grateful for the fact that:

a) I was dating someone who was thoughtful enough to plan this for me, and

b) I was in Napa—how could I not be grateful?

While the trip wasn't hiccup free by any stretch of the imagination, it was perfectly imperfect and, naturally, there was *a lot* of wine. The most insane thing about it? My poolside vision of me running through the vineyards came true. Details: they matter. I don't think I've ever been so happy. I was literally high on life and even higher on our epic love that was blooming faster than lilies in June. I was completely and totally in the moment, loving the sunshine, the wine, the Jeep we were in, the little Airbnb we were staying at, everything. I was so grateful.

**The attitude of gratitude is something the Universe loves to see.** Gratitude is being thankful for *ev-er-y-thing.* Unfortunately, feeling uber grateful all day, every day, for the rest of your life is not only unrealistic, it is impossible when your life isn't remotely close to where you want it to be. As a former naysayer and bad attitude-er, I was V. unimpressed with my life. For a long time, I was really, really (I mean, *really*) mad. Sure, I could appear happy to those around me, but on the inside? I was completely furious. I remember thinking how it wasn't fair, how life was crappy, and wondering how God or the Universe (or whatever the hell you believe in, if anything) could allow this to happen to *me* more than once.

Did I have a right to be upset? Undoubtedly.

Did I have a right to stay upset? Mmmm . . . not really. Unless, of course, I wanted to grow up to be the overly irritable old lady all the neighborhood kids are terrified of.

Yet for years, I operated under that very idea, not realizing that

I was heading straight for that not-so-ideal fate of being the old lady everyone is not-so-secretly scared of. What I didn't realize at the time, and that (thankfully) I have since learned, is my bad attitude was only attracting more and more crummy things. I was like "My life sucks so much!" and the Universe was all, "Oh, you think your miraculous life full of so much goodness and abundance isn't enough? Okay, well, if you say so . . ." and wouldn't you know, more negative things came my way—at least I perceived it all to be bad because my attitude was so negative. Like attracts like. Negative attracts negative. Positive attracts positive. Thoughts about a crappy life attract more of said crappy life. As we learned in chapter 20, if you think your life sucks, it's always going to suck.

When I made the commitment to, you know, change my life for the better, I also decided I needed to change what I was taking in on a regular basis. My self-help book collection skyrocketed. I watched *The Secret* on repeat instead of the evening news. And, instead of following influencers on Instagram who made me feel like I needed to buy a new wardrobe in order to feel better about myself, I started following people who not only were super successful but also believed the power of the Universal Laws would help get them where they wanted to be. No longer was my feed filled with friends, fitness influencers, and fellow bad attitude-ers. Instead, it was jam-packed with spiritual gurus, successful male and female powerhouses, and a bunch of other people who made me think, "Wow. I want to be like that someday."

Unfortunately, my life didn't look remotely similar to their lives, which were filled with expensive cars, luxury vacations, and attitudes that definitely didn't worry about how much groceries were going to cost that week (or ever again, for that matter). So, when my Instagram feed was filled with affirmations of "Be Grateful!" "Practice Gratitude!" and "The Attitude of Gratitude!" I wanted to scoff "You've gotta be fucking kidding me!" at my virtual internet buds.

Of course, *she's* grateful! She drives a brand-new Range Rover, has published a gazillion best-selling books, travels the world, and makes boatloads of moolah. Look at *him*! He has everything you could ever want. I mean, what's not to be grateful for? But here's the thing: I was so focused on what I didn't have that I never took a look around to realize what I *did* have. And, FYI, I'm not just referring to material possessions.

First of all, not to sound dramatic, but I was alive, healthy, and breathing. We often take our health for granted until we lose it altogether; but in reality, just being able to see clearly, breathe deeply, and walk around this beautiful planet of ours is something to be super grateful for. I was able to graduate from college after seven roller-coaster years (yes, the top of her high school class took *se-ven* years to graduate). I had overcome super-traumatic and life-altering events. Talk about strength. Talk about some serious resilience for someone who hadn't been alive for even three decades. I had my own apartment and a dog whose mere existence made me smile. Sure, I had to live off ramen noodles from the dollar store (and I had to pay with coins), but I was lucky enough to have those things. How freakin' amazing is that? Not everyone in the world gets such a precious opportunity. I had a bed to sleep in, clothes to wear, and two legs to get me to where I needed to be.

I had *enough.*

Even though I had been taking for granted almost every single thing I had, the Universe always made sure I had enough. I just never realized it. So, I decided to take the advice of all those internet gurus and try a little experiment. I started looking at everything around me as if it were covered in gold and had angels with harps dancing all around it. Okay, I *might* be exaggerating a little bit here, but I did go out of my way to be grateful for everything around me, no matter how seemingly unimportant it was. I was thankful there was traffic. I was thankful when I had to wait in line at the grocery store while the person in front of me paid in coins. Don't get me wrong: I wasn't *always* feeling thankful. But I did make a point to return to a feeling of gratitude once I let myself experience any negative emotion that came up. And wouldn't you know it, my good ole Instagram friends actually knew what the hell they were talking about. While a brand-new, luxury SUV didn't appear in my garage and I still had to think about the cost of groceries, I was immediately, and I mean, *im-med-i-ate-ly* happier. Like, genuinely happy—not the fake kind of happy I had been projecting for over a decade. Instead of thinking about how much my life sucked and how I didn't deserve to be hurt so badly, I thought about how lucky I was to even survive and how *grateful* I was to get so far from where I started. And the Universe was like, "Okay. *Now* you get it. Here's some more of where that came from!" and amazing things poured into my life as if some sort of metaphorical good-stuff-r-us floodgates burst open.

Although I wish it were different, there will be bad things that happen to you or days when you're in a funk, for a reason or for no reason at all. We're human. We can't be blissfully happy 24/7, 365. However, if you actively try to focus on things/people/dogs/whatever it is that you're grateful for (instead of getting all up in arms and seeing red), you'll feel an immediate change in your spirit. You'll feel lighter. You'll feel . . . good. And doesn't it feel really good to feel really good? Let me answer this one for you: Yes. It feels damn good, and we all deserve to feel damn good!

Gratitude increases your vibration. A high vibe attracts more high vibe things—and I'm assuming your biggest goals and dreams are operating on a pretty elevated energetic frequency. Being super thankful for what you already have is one thing; being grateful for what you want when you don't have it yet is on another level. This not only shows the Universe that you are a green light for your desires, but your vibration is through the metaphorical roof. How can you be grateful for what you want when it doesn't exist in your (physical) reality? By acting as if you *already* have it. Embody the version of you who has it all. How would you act if what you wanted was already yours? How would you be dressed? How would you respond to unexpected left turns? This goes back to what we learned in chapter 24: your faith in the Universe should be so unwavering that nothing can deter you from your dreams. Let's pretend you want a million dollars; would a millionaire scream at the veterinarian for an unexpected, large bill? I doubt it. WWTFYD: What would the future you do?

Speaking of action, there's one final V. important reminder I have for you. While ev-er-y-thing begins and ends in your mind, and it truly is the ticket to receiving ev-er-y-thing you want in this lifetime, you also usually need to take action to get there. While sometimes your mind really can do the work, sometimes you have to contribute in an inspired way. If your dream is to live in a two-bedroom apartment in New York City, you can't simply close your eyes, visualize the apartment, be super clear and grateful, and open your eyes and expect to find yourself in the middle of Manhattan. Similarly, if you want to be in the epic relationship of your dreams, you are going to have to take some action and go on dates with people. Inspired action is not forced—it flows. It comes from a place of inspiration and intuition rather than the mindset of okay-well-I-just-have-to-do-this-to-get-what-I-want-even-though-I-don't-really-want-to. Tap into your intuition, connect to your higher self, and believe that you are the version of you who already has it. This version of you does a fantastic job of feeling grateful for what is yours now and thankful for what's still to come. This version of you does not try to control the outcome; it surrenders to the Universe. This version of you *also* knows when it's time to make a move.

I warned you that this process is by no means easy. While being equally grateful for what I had and what I didn't have (yet) instantly made me feel happier, I wasn't immediately changed. I still had, you know, some stuff to digest and face head on. I had to reflect. I had to go back to the past in order to fully appreciate the present and reframe what things meant to me. While no one wants to stay in the past, it is important to reflect on it in order to acknowledge what's happened and what is working and what isn't; that way, we can, you know, change. Facing the past usually means going back down some roads that were really fucking bumpy and made us feel like we were going to throw up on the side of the road. This is where the whole forgiveness part comes in: forgiving everyone, including (most importantly) yourself. Grace is something we all deserve, but the person who needs it the most is *you*. You were just doing what you needed to do at the time to get by. That is okay. And you, my darling, are *so much more* than okay. Remember, if you don't love the fuck out of you, the Universe isn't going to send someone who will love the fuck out of you. I used to dream about meeting the guy who would save me—the guy who would make it right. But the truth is: I was the only one who could save me. I was the knight in shining armor I wanted all along. The same goes for you.

Meeting the love of your life, soulmate, or life partner isn't the happy ending. Finding *yourself*—the real you—and fiercely loving that incredible human is the ultimate goal. You see, you've been the epic love you needed all along. *You* are your happy ending. Falling in epic love with another amazing human is a (delicious) cherry on top of an already delectable ice cream sundae. It's absolutely okay to want that cherry, but don't forget that you're mouthwatering on your own.

The best part of this whole process is when you realize that *you*, of all freaking people, have had the power to make your dreams a reality all along. It's right there in between your ears; it's your mind. When you get your mind right, everything will change; you will realize that no matter what you face, you're going to get through it because you are always on the right path and the Universe is always there to help you. When you realize you can ask for anything you want and you'll either get it or something way better and aligned with your highest good, **you hold the power to not only survive, but to thrive.**

When you can leave the past in the past and surrender to the Universe, be happy with what you already have, and feel wickedly grateful for what you want as though it's already yours, that's the ticket to forever. Are you satisfied with what is? What *can* you be satisfied with? Look around. You have a lot to be grateful for, even if it's the tiny things. Start with tiny and work your way up from there. The Universe will respond tenfold. The Universe wants you to be happy. I want you to be happy. You deserve to be happy and have everything your heart desires whether it's a life partner, self-confidence, Enrique Iglesias in your bed, epic love, or to be confident in bed with your epic love who happens to be Enrique Iglesias's long-lost twin brother (or fraternal twin sister). Whatever it is, it *can* be yours. Beyond simply being grateful for what is, it's imperative to be grateful for what you want as though you've already got it. It not only shows your unwavering belief and trust in the Universe, but also that you have truly surrendered.

The Universe believes in you. I believe in you. It's time for *you* to believe in you.

# Afterword—
# The Moment I Realized I Was the Girl on Fire after All

*Nothing can dim the light which shines from within.*
*—Maya Angelou*

Some people say that there are only two certainties in life: death and taxes. I'd like to add a third to the list: adversity. We've all been through some sort of adversity and will likely face challenges in the future. This is a fact of life: it's never going to be perfect. Of course, we'll have moments of perfection mixed in with moments of imperfection. We will experience failure, success, and everything in between. We aren't meant to simply survive this wild ride we've been blessed with on this planet. We are meant to *thrive*, despite all the adversity we have faced in the past and will face in the future.

The most important realization I came to during my journey to falling in epic love with my life was that I was way more like Katniss Everdeen than I thought—*and you are too.* Like Katniss, we can often be wildly misunderstood. But how can we be fully understood by anyone who doesn't know all of our thoughts, dreams, hopes, fears, regrets, wins, and failures as intimately as we do? This is just one of the reasons you need to love the fuck out of yourself, first and foremost: no one will ever be able to understand you better than you.

Unlike Katniss, we might not be warriors who are a crack shot with a bow and arrow, and we certainly aren't fictional characters from a bestselling book series, but we are still warriors in our own right. Throughout *The Hunger Games* series, Katniss stays true to herself despite overwhelming evidence suggesting that she should change to please others (and to, well, save a lot of lives). She goes to hell and back, survives it all, and comes out on the other side, even stronger and more true to herself than when she started.

Was Katniss universally liked? No way. Did it matter? Not at all. What matters most is if *you* like you—not if the rest of the population feels the same way. Remember: your sole purpose is not to be loved by everyone around you. You're here to light up your own path—a path no one *but* you could possibly illuminate in such a beautiful way.

Does Katniss make mistakes along the way? Uh, yeah she does. Does she have epic losses and unbelievable successes? Totally. Were there times she felt like there was no freaking way she'd survive? I don't know about you, but if I were in a real-life version of *The Hunger Games*, there would probably be a lot of moments when I would think, well, this is finally *it*; however, while hardship and adversity are inevitable, it doesn't mean your life has to end as you know it. You are a living, breathing miracle who has everything you have ever needed, even when it feels like you have no choice but to give up.

While we might not all have the unwavering confidence and physical capabilities of Miss Everdeen, we all hold the power within ourselves to come out on top. Your *internal* strength is one of your many superpowers. **You are the superhero of your life, and you don't need anyone but *yourself* to save you.**

There will inevitably be moments, days, weeks, years, or even decades when it feels like you can't possibly get through it. You're going to face epic challenges. You're going to be scared, overwhelmed, and all-of-the-things. No matter how awful things have been for you in the past and no matter what struggle you are going through now, don't let it steer you into the darkness for good. I promise you this: you *can*, and you *will* get through it. When you find yourself forgetting this fact, **reclaim your inner fire.**

We're all on fire, lighting our own way on our own paths. Each path goes in its own direction, but we all have everything we need to succeed in every area of life—epically romantic love life included. *You* are everything you have ever needed. When you are feeling lost or facing the most challenging of adversities, remember to look inside and fuel the fire within yourself. You've been on fire all this time—go ahead and fan your flame.

# Acknowledgements

To my husband, Basil (who found out about this book *weeks* after meeting me, read it, and decided I was his person anyway), if I had to go through all the heartbreak over again in order to meet you, I'd do it. Thank you for your endless support and love, for providing affirmations when I need them most, and for filling my wine glass without being asked. I hope everyone meets their own Basil.

Mom and Dad, I sincerely hope this is the only page you read from this book. Thank you for believing in me when I forgot to believe in myself. I wouldn't be here without you (literally . . . and figuratively).

Kira, thank you for never judging me during my decade of questionable dating decisions. Your warmth, guidance, love, and ability to make me do things I'm terrified of are just a few of the things I cherish about you. I'm so happy you found your forever.

Ari, you are the best older sister that I never had. Thank you for being there for me during the low moments, celebrating with me during the high moments, and for always being down to drink another glass of rosé.

Kris, thank you for agreeing to read my first couple of chapters years ago when I told you I was writing a "little something." Without your encouragement, I would have given up. I also have to thank you for introducing me to *Magic Mike Live* and for inspiring me every day.

Randi, thank you for agreeing to go with me on the best/worst weekend trip of all time and forcing me to text *Mr. East Coast* for clarity, even though his response was (unsurprisingly) cold and heartbreaking. You're always my number one hype girl, and I appreciate that more than you know.

Louise, you are the best friend I have never met (although, I do hope that changes one day). There is no doubt in my mind the Universe was involved the day I commented on your Instagram photo. Thank you for the relentless encouragement and for sharing your publishing knowledge. I can't wait for the day when our books sit together on the same shelf.

Alison, boy did you have a tall order in editing this book! Thank you for helping me rein things in when I needed to (which was more often than not) and for making my words—and my story—that much more powerful.

To all the men in this book, thank you. Thank you for (almost) breaking me because through that pain I found myself, learned to love her fiercely, and reclaimed my inner fire—and that's the greatest gift of all.

Finally, to the awesome Universe, thank you for the lessons, the unwavering love, and the signs when I needed them. I'll never look at pineapples the same way again.

With so much gratitude,
Mikaela

# About the Author

Mikaela Kostaras spent over a decade planning weddings, teaching and competing in ballroom dance, and establishing a career in Hospitality Sales. Despite her seemingly successful work life, she was miserable—she hated men and she hated her life.

So, she embarked on an expedition to find and heal her most authentic self, ultimately becoming a reformed serial fuckboy dater and trauma survivor (and thriver). Her journey to fuckboy freedom allowed her to escape the dating scene and manifest the man of her dreams, to whom she is now happily married.

Mikaela's success in manifesting her dreams didn't stop with her husband. She was able to leave her corporate career behind and step into her purpose and passion full-time: inspiring others to do the same for themselves—especially through writing!

She writes weekly on her blog, which focuses on self-love, mindset, and not-your-garden-variety dating advice without too much yawn-inducing preachiness (though there's definitely a boatload of inspiration). You could call her the "salt bae of self-love," sprinkling nuggets of wisdom and encouragement everywhere she goes.

Mikaela's refreshingly witty and candid voice breaks down the most woo-wooey of spiritual ideas into easily accessible concepts and offers examples everyone can relate to.

She lives in Scottsdale, Arizona with her handsome husband and sassy German Shepherd, Maya. You can usually find her reading inspiring books, watching Formula 1 or Netflix, working out, and drinking red wine. This doesn't usually happen all at the same time, although there have been a few occasions.

Made in the USA
Columbia, SC
25 September 2021

46091962R00148